UNDERSTANDING EXTENSION EDUCATION

UNDERSTANDING EXTENSION EDUCATION

Maimun Nisha

KALPAZ

Published by

Kalpaz Publications
C-30, Satyawati Nagar,
Delhi – 110052
Ph.: 011-47034999, 9811692060
www.kalpazpublications.com
E-mail: kalpaz@hotmail.com

Distribution Network
gyanbooks.com
India, USA, Canada, UK, Australia, France

ISBN: 978-81-7835-495-8 (HB)

Reprint in India, 2024
First Published, 2006

Printed at: Gyan Press, Delhi.

Understanding Extension Education
Author: Maimun Nisha

Contents

Preface 9

1. **Understanding Extension Education** 11
Introduction • The Concept of Extension • Knowledge and Skills • Technical Advice and Information • Farmers' Organization • Motivation and Self-confidence • Importance of Extension • Knowledge ↔ Communication ↔ Farm Family • Principles of Extension • Types of Extension • Methods of Extension Education • Differences between Formal Education and Extension Education • Need of Extension Education • Scope of Extension Education • Importance of Extension Education • Objectives of Extension Education • Principles of Extension Education • Philosophy of Exten-sion Education • Community Development • Community Development (Now Rural Development) and Extension Service in India • Extension Education System • Early Efforts in Rural Reconstruction.

2. **Extension Educational Psychology** 57
Concepts of Extension Educational Psychology • Steps in Extension Teaching • Principles of Learning • Learning Situation • Factors Effecting Adult Learning • Educational Psychology

• Nature of Educational Psychology • Adult Education • Teaching • Factors Affect on Teaching • Learning Experiences.

3. **Communication of Innovation** 71
Communication • Act of Communication • The Four Elements of Communication • Listening • Shared Meanings • Mass Media in Extension • Audio-visual Aids in Extension • What is Innovation? • The Origin of Innovation • Definition of Innovation • Adoption Curves • Categories of Adopters • Characteristics of Adopters • Characteristics of Innovations • Stages of the Adoption Process • Diffusion of Innovation Theory • Definition of Diffusion of Innovation • Diffusion of Innovation • Characteristics Adopters • The Adoption Process • Five Stages of Adoption • The Innovation-Decision Process • Five Stages of the Diffusion Process • Innovation Decision Process • Innovativeness and Adopter Categories • Rate of Adoption.

4. **Extension Teaching Methods** 97
Selection of Methods • Selection of Methods • Programme Delivery Methods • A Programme Delivery System • Programme Delivery Methods • Reinforcement Methods • Information about Instructional Methods • Lecture-cum-Discussion • Discussion • Small Group Discussion • Lecture • Lecture with Discussion • Panel of Experts • Brainstorming • Videotapes • Class Discussion • Small Group Discussion • Case Studies • Role Playing • Report-Back Sessions • Worksheets/Surveys • Index and Exercise • Guest Speaker • Values Classification Exercise • Teaching with Slides • Presentation Technology • Video and Film • Designating

Roles in Groups • Reporting Group Results • Teaching with the Case Method • Formats for Cases • Managing a Case Assignment • Designing Case Study Questions • Managing Discussion and Debate Effectively • Organizing the Groups • Designating Roles in Groups • Reporting Group Results • Lecturing • Planning a Lecture • Analyzing the Audience • Generating an Outline • Choosing Examples • Choosing Learning Activities • Reviewing the Material • Delivering the Lecture • Questioning in the Classroom • Answering Students' Questions • Teaching Outside Your Field of Specialization • Extension Methods • Individual Methods of Extension • Farm Visits • Planning the Visit • Making the Visit • Office Calls • Letters • Individual Methods • Group Methods of Extension • Advantages of Group Methods • Coverage • Learning Environment • Action • Important Issues in Group Extension • Agent's Relationship with Group • Types of Group Extension Methods • Form of the Meeting • Planning the Meeting • Conducting the Meeting • Demonstrations • Method Demonstration • Result Demonstration • Basic Principles for Demonstrations • Planning the Demonstration • Preparing the Demonstration • Supervising the Demonstration • Follow-up • Field Days • Tours • Public Speaking • Mass Media in Extension • Audio-visual Aids in Extension • The Range of Audio-visual Aids • Using Audio-visual Aids • Relative Effectiveness of Methods.

5. **Extension Programme Planning** 185

Extension Programmes • Extension Programmes bring Together National Policies and

Local Initiatives • Process in Programme Planning • 1. Situation Analysis • 2. Setting Objectives • 3. Developing an Extension Programme • 4. Implementation • 5. Evaluation • Evaluating Extension Programmes • Levels of Evaluation • Importance of Extension Programme • Characteristics of Programme Planning • Organizations Involvement in Planning an Extension Programme • Setting the Objective of the Programme • The Desired Change • Evaluating the Programme • Choosing and Using the Media • Organizing a Seminar • Refreshment • Recording • Discussion Groups • Organizing a Discussion Group • Field Days • Organizing A Field Day • Organizing a Workshop • Organizing a Radio Talk • Planning, Preparation, Practice and Poise or Confidence • Organizing a Newsletter • Organizing an Article • People Involvement in Programme Planning • Government Involvement in Programme Planning • Development Planning

6. **Extension Administration** 251

Introduction • How to Develop Extension Organization • Goal of Extension Organisation • Concept of Extension Organisation • Principles of Administration • Technical Problems in Building of an Organization • Extension Adminstration • Efficiency in Administration

7. **Rural Sociology** 263

Introduction • Meaning • Rural Institutions • Clubs for Rural Youth • Projects with Rural Youth • Development of Rural Sociology • Principles of Rural Development Programmes • Extension Cooperates with Other Rural

Development Organizations • Social and Cultural Factors in Extension • Social Groups • Culture • Farming Systems • Farming Systems • Social and Cultural Change • Factors in Change • Social and Cultural Barriers to Agricultural Change.

8. **Community Organization** **295**
The Role of the Agent • Knowledge ↔ Communication ↔ Innovation • Educator ↔ Facilitator ↔ Catalyst • Knowledge and Personal Skills • Methods of Community Organization.

Bibliography 317

Index 319

Preface

It is a great pleasure to note that "Understanding Extension Education" will be popular among the students who are looking for the results in this cut-throat world.

This book closely follows the syllabus prescribed by the universities in extension education and home science.

The problem of extension development is the essence of the process of economic development in India. Rural India covers 75 per cent of the total population. Writers efforts to eradicate poverty and provide tools and techniques in the absolute sense.

This book analyses the way, methods, techniques, philosophy, principles in which the extension education can help to removal of poverty and bring about an integrated rural development in India. In this perspective the necessity of having a new definition of extension education has been felt. The new definition does not envisage rural development as ends in themselves but a means to realize our long cherished and of uplifting rural India and villagers. These extension education are expected to bring about a better interaction between agriculture, rural sociology, farmers, rural administrators and thereby become effective instrument of rural development on sound lines.

This strategy appears to be an improvement over the existing one insofar as the former has the promise of making the process of rural and extension development.

This book represents the concept, principle, philosophy, objective, method, rural problems, rural training, rural administration, programme planning, village workers, village agriculture, etc.

The book title shows it is a primary book of Extension Education for the students of university classes.

This book is helpful them and covers the all chapters and courses of the universities, department of agriculture, Home Science, and dairy.

This book is beneficent to that student who want to established their carrier in village, to help the rural people and provide the village programmes.

This book also helpful the student who will research in rural areas in future.

This book "Understanding the Extension Education" is help the village workers, village leaders, programme planners, gram sevaks and sevikas, community development officers, extension worker.

This book should be of use not only the students as a text book but also to the teacher of extension education departments.

Maimun Nisha

1

Understanding Extension Education

Introduction

The term extension was first used in the United States of America in the first decade of this century to connote the extension of knowledge from the Land Grant Colleges to the farmers through the process of informal education. In India, the terms community development and extension education became more popular with the launching of Community Development Projects in 1952 and with the establishment of the National Extension Service in 1953. Since then, Community development has been regarded as a programme for an all-round development of the rural people, and extension education as the means to achieve this objective. Extension education is an applied behavioural science the knowledge of which is applied to bring about desirable changes in the behavioural complex of human beings usually through various strategies and programmes of change and by applying the latest scientific and technological innovations.

Extension education has now developed as a full-fledged discipline, having its own philosophy objectives, principles, methods and techniques which must be understood by every extension worker and others connected with the rural development. It might be mentioned here that extension education, its principles, methods and techniques are applicable not only to agriculture but also to veterinary and animal husbandry, dairying, home science, health, family planning, etc. Based upon its application and use, various nomenclatures have been given to it, such as agricultural extension veterinary and animal husbandry extension, dairy extension, home science extension public health extension, and family planning extension.

Extension means to spread, to use, to supply useful informations to rural people, schools, and colleges regularly. Through these, changes bring out in the society. Extension education is very necessary for rural people outside the organised schools, classrooms for bringing out social and cultural development. Extension education develop the social behavioural pattern of the human being and different social groups.

Extension education helps to decrease the gap created by culture. Extension education has broad scope and a educational programme for rural people, which solve problems on self-help basis. It is a learning and teaching process which bring out these types of charges in human behaviour:

(1) Change in knowledge.

(2) Changes in skills.

(3) Changes in attitudes.

The Concept of Extension

The concept and practice of extension are the central themes of this guide. However, before beginning to look at the many different aspects of extension practice in later chapters, the meaning of the term extension needs to be examined. Rural extension is now a common activity in most countries of the world, and it is a basic element in programmes and projects formulated to bring about change in rural areas. Extension services are similarly a common feature of the administrative structure of rural areas and these services have the responsibility, in partnership with the farmers, of directing programmes and projects for change.

Extension is a term which is open to a wide variety of interpretations. Each extension agent probably has his own understanding of what extension is. This understanding will be based on past experience and the particular type of extension service in which the agent is working. In other words, there is no single definition of extension which is universally accepted or which is applicable to all situations. Furthermore, extension is a dynamic concept in the sense that the interpretation of it is always changing. Extension, therefore, is not a term which can be precisely defined, but one which describes a continual and changing process in rural areas.

The term extension may be examined by looking at a number of statements that have been written in this

- Extension is an informal educational process directed toward the rural population. This process offers advice and information to help them solve their problems. Extension also aims to increase the efficiency of the family farm, increase production and generally increase the standard of living of the farm family.

- The objective of extension is to change farmers' outlook toward their difficulties. Extension is concerned not just with physical and economic achievements but also with the development of the rural people themselves. Extension agents, therefore, discuss matters with the rural people, help them to gain a clearer insight into their problems and also to decide how to overcome these problems.

> Extension is a process of working with rural people in order to improve their livelihoods. This involves helping farmers to improve the productivity of their agriculture and also developing their abilities to direct their own future development.

The above statements are presented to illustrate the range of interpretations that can be found about extension. They do, however, contain a number of common points. They all stress that extension is a process which occurs over a period of time, and not a single, one-time activity. They also all underline extension as an educational process which works with rural people, supports them and prepares them to confront their problems more successfully.

If statements such as those above are examined more carefully, and if the current ideas and practice of extension are considered, four main elements can be identified within the process of extension: knowledge and skills, technical advice and information, farmers' organization, and motivation and self-confidence.

Knowledge and Skills

Although farmers already have a lot of knowledge about their environment and their farming system, extension can bring them other knowledge and information which they do not have. For example, knowledge about the cause of the damage to a particular crop, the general principles of pest control, or the ways in which manure and compost are broken down to provide plant nutrients are all areas of knowledge that the agent can usefully bring to farmers.

The application of such knowledge often means that the farmer has to acquire new skills of various kinds: for example, technical skills to operate unfamiliar equipment, organizational skills to manage a group project, the skill to assess the economic aspects of technical advice given, or farm management skills for keeping records and allocating the use of farm resources and equipment.

The transfer of knowledge and skills to farmers and their families is an important extension activity and the extension agent must prepare himself thoroughly. He must find out which skills or areas of knowledge are lacking among the farmers in his area, and then arrange suitable learning experiences through which the farmers can acquire them.

Technical Advice and Information

Extension also provides advice and information to assist farmers in making decisions and generally enable them to take action. This can be information about prices and markets, for example, or about the availability of credit and inputs. The technical advice will probably apply more directly to the production activities of the family farm and to the action needed to improve or sustain this production. Much of this technical advice will be based upon the findings of agricultural research. In many instances, however, farmers are also sources of valuable advice and information for other farmers, and agents should always try to establish a farmer-to-farmer link.

Farmers' Organization

As well as knowledge, information and technical advice, farmers also need some form of organization, both to represent their interests and to give them a means for taking collective action. Extension, therefore, should be concerned with helping to set up, structure and develop organizations of local farmers. This should be a joint venture and any such organization should only be set up in consultation with the farmers. In the future, these organizations will make it easier for extension services to work with local farmers, and will also serve as a channel for disseminating information and knowledge.

Motivation and Self-confidence

One of the main constraints to development that many farmers face is isolation, and a feeling that there is little they can do to change their lives. Some farmers will have spent all their lives struggling in difficult circumstances to provide for their families with little support or encouragement. It is important for extension to work closely with farmers, helping them to take the initiative and generally encouraging them to become involved in extension activities. Equally important is to convince farmers that they can do things for themselves, that they can make decisions and that they have the ability to break out of their poverty.

The above are the four fundamental elements of the extension process. It is not suggested that all extension activities must contain each of these elements, nor that some are more important than others. Clearly, the extension approach will be determined by the particular circumstances. However, an overall extension service should be based on these elements and should seek to promote them within the rural areas. Sometimes the local farmers problems will demand prompt information and advice; on other occasions, more patient work of organization and motivation may be required. An extension service must be able to respond to these different demands.

Importance of Extension

Within the framework presented in this chapter, the concept and practice of the central issue of this guide must now be examined: extension work in rural communities. Extension is essentially the means by which new knowledge and ideas are introduced into rural areas in order to bring about change and improve the lives of farmers and their families. Extension, therefore, is of critical importance. Without it farmers would lack access to the support and services required to improve their agriculture and other productive activities. The critical importance of extension can be understood better if its three main elements are considered:

Knowledge ↔ Communication ↔ Farm Family

Extension is not concerned directly with generating knowledge; that is done in specialized institutions such as agricultural research centers, agricultural colleges or engineering departments. Extension takes this knowledge and makes it available to the farm family. Rural extension, therefore, is the process whereby knowledge is communicated, in a variety of ways, to the farm family. This process is usually guided and supported by an extension agent who works at the programme and project level, and who is in direct contact with farmers and their families.

To do this extension work, agents have to be trained in the different aspects of the extension process. One aspect of this training is giving the agent the technical or scientific knowledge required for the job. This is usually done during the agent's professional training; however, it is only one element in the process. The other two elements of the process are equally important. It is not enough for an extension agent to have technical knowledge; he must also know-how to communicate this knowledge and how to use it to the benefit of the farm family. Training in extension, therefore, is an equally important aspect of the training of any agent who wishes to work with farmers.

Principles of Extension

Extension activities are widespread throughout the developing world and most governments have set up formally structured extension services to implement extension programmes and projects. The practice of extension is supported by budget, offices, personnel and other resources. Before examining extension in detail in later chapters, however, it will be useful to consider the principles which should guide it.

Extension Works with People

Extension works with rural people. Only the people themselves can make decisions about the way they will farm or live and an extension agent does not try to take these decisions for them. Rural people can and do make wise decisions about their problems if they are given full information including possible alternative solutions. By making decisions, people gain self-confidence. Extension, therefore, presents facts, helps people to solve problems and encourages farmers to make decisions. People have more confidence in programmes and decisions which they have made themselves than in those which are imposed upon them.

Extension is Accountable to its Clients

Extension services and agents have two sets of masters. On the one hand, they are accountable to their senior officers and to the government departments that determine rural development policies. Agents are expected to follow official policies and guidelines in their work.

On the other hand, extension is the servant of the rural people and it has the responsibility to fulfill the needs of the people in its area. This means that the rural poor should have a say in deciding how effective extension actually is. One measure of effectiveness is to see how well policies and plans have been carried out. An equally important measure is the extent to which incomes and living standards of the rural people have increased as a result of extension work.

Extension programmes, therefore, are based on people's needs, as well as on technical and national economic needs. The extension agent's task is to bring these needs together. For example, an important part of government policy may be to increase the amount of food grown and sold in the country. By choosing to encourage the mass of small farmers to increase their output by improving their farming methods, national needs and farmers' needs can be satisfied together.

Extension is a Two-Way Link

Extension is not a one-way process in which the extension agent transfers knowledge and ideas to farmers and their families. Such advice, which is often based upon the findings of agricultural and other research stations, is certainly important but the flow of information from farmers to extension and research workers is equally important. Extension should be ready to receive farmers' ideas, suggestions or advice, as well as to give them. This two-way flow of ideas can occur at different stages.

When the problem is being defined. Being in regular contact with the farmers, the extension agent can help research workers to understand the farming problems of the area and the limitations under which farmers have to work. It is even better if the agent can bring researchers into direct contact with farmers in order to ensure that research recommendations are relevant to farmers' needs.

Extension Links Farmers with Research

When recommendations are being tested in the field. A new farm practice or crop variety might produce good results at a research station but not do so well on a farmer's field. Trials on farmers' fields are an opportunity to test research recommendations and provide feedback for research staff.

When farmers put recommendations into practice. Sometimes farmers discover problems with a recommendation which the research station failed to note. With the feedback the recommendations can be adjusted accordingly.

The two-way link between research, extension and the farmer is fundamental to sound extension practice and should be a basic principle of extension activity.

Extension Cooperates with Other Rural Development Organizations

Within rural areas, extension services and agents should work closely with the other organizations that provide essential services to farmers and their families. Extension is only one aspect of the many economic, social and political activities that seek to produce change for the better in rural society. Extension, therefore, must be prepared to collaborate with all other such organizations, both government and non-government, and to take them into account when preparing to implement extension policies. The kinds of organizations with which extension services should cooperate include:

Political institutions and local political leaders whose active local support will help the extension agent, who may thereby be brought into closer touch with local farmers.

Support organizations such as those which supply agricultural or other inputs, credit facilities or marketing services. Such inputs must be available in sufficient quantity, in the right place and at the right time if they are to be of any use.

Health services, so that the extension agent is kept aware of local health problems, particularly nutritional levels. Agricultural development and nutrition are closely related and the agent must keep closely in touch with health programmes and projects and adapt his programme to conform to local health requirements.

Local schools, so that the agent can have early access to the farmers of the future, and begin to equip them with the knowledge and skills required for farming.

Community development, whose objectives will be very similar to the educational work of extension. Extension agents often work very closely with community development workers to breakdown local social and cultural barriers to change, and to encourage community action programmes.

It is essential that the extension agent in the field know what his colleagues in other services and government departments are doing, and that they understand what he is doing. Close cooperation not only avoids duplication but provides opportunities for integrated farm programmes.

Extension Works with Different Target Groups

Extension recognizes that not all farmers in any one area will have the same problems. Some will have more land than others and will be keen to try out new ideas. Others, with fewer resources, will probably be more cautious. Extension cannot offer a single "package" of advice, suitable to all farmers. Different groups need to be identified and the agent will have to develop programmes appropriate to each group.

In the past, much extension effort was concentrated on the progressive farmer who was expected to spread new ideas to others. It has been seen, however, that this does not always work, because progressive farmers often have different problems. They have more land, more education and are usually more involved in the marketing of their produce.

Extension must, therefore, be aware of the existence of different farming groups and plan its programmes accordingly. The smallest and poorest farmers will need particular attention, as they may lack the basic resources needed to become involved in extension activities. The point to stress, therefore, is the existence of farmer groups with different resources and skills in any one community, and the need for extension to respond to these groups accordingly.

Types of Extension

There is no one universal type of extension but a variety of activities and approaches which can be called extension. It has already been stated that since agriculture is the basis of a rural economy, agricultural extension is the most common type of extension to be found in rural areas. But the areas of knowledge and new ideas that farmers and their families require are not restricted to agriculture. There are other aspects of family life in which new knowledge and practices can lead to improvement. Extension is any activity that works with farmers and their families in order to improve the economic and social conditions of their lives and to develop their ability to take responsibility for their own future development. This extension, however, can take different forms and it would be useful to review the two principal ones.

Agricultural Extension

There are probably more extension agents involved in agricultural activities than in any other aspect of rural life. Given the importance of agriculture and the need to produce food both for the farm family and for the nation as a whole, this emphasis upon agricultural extension is understandable. Some agricultural extension services are based upon a single crop, while others adopt more of a "whole farm" approach. The choice is very much dependent upon the local agricultural system and the national crop requirements. In regions where cash crops such as cotton, cocoa or sugar grow, the single crop extension approach is more common.

An agricultural extension service offers technical advice on agriculture to farmers, and also supplies them with the necessary inputs and services to support their agricultural production. It provides information to farmers and passes to the farmers new ideas developed by agricultural research stations. Agricultural extension programmes cover a broad area including improved crop varieties, better livestock control, improved water management, and the control of weeds, pests or plant diseases. Where appropriate, agricultural extension may also help to build up local farmers' groups and organizations so that they can benefit from extension programmes. Agricultural extension, therefore, provides the indispensable elements that farmers need to improve their agricultural productivity.

Non-agriculural Extension

In the absence of a collective term to cover the other types of extension, it is convenient to refer to them all as non-agricultural extension. This term includes all activities and efforts not directly related to agriculture or livestock production, but which are important to the farm families. Home economics, family health and nutrition, population education and community development are all non-agricultural extension activity.

Rural Extension Covers Many Aspects of Rural Life

When talking of extension and extension agents, therefore, all activities of the above type are included. These activities also involve the basic elements and principles of extension outlined earlier in this chapter, such as knowledge, learning and practice. Home economists and community development workers, therefore, are extension agents who deal with farm families in the same way as agricultural extension agents. The only difference is their areas of concern.

In fact, it is becoming increasingly common to talk of rural extension as a collective term which brings together all agricultural and non-agricultural extension activities. The feature common to both types of extension is that they work with families in rural areas and deal with problems in a rural environment. Their different programmes and approaches have a common aim, which is the improvement of the lives of the rural people, and they are both guided by common principles and ideals.

This guide, therefore, is a guide to rural extension and is relevant to both agricultural and non-agricultural extension agents. Given the predominance of agriculture in the rural economy, however, there will be some emphasis on agricultural extension within the guide. The understanding of extension, the methods used by extension agents, the planning processes involved and the qualities and skills required by agents are factors relevant to all forms of rural extension. The content and subject-matter may be different, but the same general principles apply in both types of extension.

Methods of Extension Education

Extension education involves three methods namely:

(a) Informal education.

(b) Formal education.

(c) Non-formal education.

Informal Education: It is a very lengthy life long education process and which acquires knowledge, skill, attitude and insights from daily experiences at home, work, play, fear groups, books journals and television.

Formal Education: It is very organization based, chronologically graded hierarchically structured educational system from learner primary school to university level education.

Non-formal Education: It is systematic organised education system but different from formal education system which provide selected learning process in population for adult and children. If provide education for agriculture, extension, farmers, training programmes, adult literacy programmes, community programmes, health programme, nutrition programme, family planning etc.

General education based an formal education methods, form lower primary children to youth. This programmes also include in extension education.

Differences between Formal Education and Extension Education

It may, however, be mentioned here that when extension education is put into action for educating the rural people, it does not remain formal education. In that sense there are several differences between the two. Some of these differences are:

Formal Education	*Extension Education*
1. The teacher starts with theory and works up to practicals.	1. The teacher (extension worker) starts with practicals and may take up theory later on.
2. Students study subjects.	2. Farmers study problems.
3. Students must adapt themselves to the fixed curriculum offered.	3. It has no fixed curriculum or course of study and the farmers help to formulate the curriculum.
4. Authority rests with the teacher.	4. Authority rests with the farmers.
5. Class attendance is compulsory.	5. Participation is voluntary.
6. Teacher instructs the students.	6. Teacher teaches and also learns from the farmers.
7. Teaching is only through instructors.	7. Teaching is also through local leaders.
8. Teaching is mainly vertical.	8. Teaching is mainly horizontal.
9. The teacher has more or less homogeneous audience.	9. The teacher has a large and heterogeneous audience.
10. It is rigid.	10. It is flexible.
11. It has all pre-planned and predecided programme.	11. It has freedom to develop programmes locally and they are expressed desires of the people.
12. It is more theoretical.	12. It is more practical and application in the solution of problems.

Need of Extension Education

The need is very essential for farmers because:

(a) Extension education supplied recent and useful informations to agriculture.

(b) It provide latest technology.

(c) It provide knowledge to adopt new scientific methods.

(d) It develop the ability of the farmers.

(e) It equipped the farmers for jobs.

(f) It carry the problems of farmers to the research stations for solutions.

(g) It provide agency to import the finding of new research.

(h) It fulfil the gap of extension agency.

Scope of Extension Education

The scope of extension education totally based on the development of the rural people, for changing the conditions. Constantly of the villagers through dynamic approaches and excellent scientific programmes. The following areas include in scope of extension work in rural areas:

1. Enhance the quality of agricultural production.
2. Enhance the efficiency in marketing distribution and utilisation of agricultural inputs and outputs.
3. Increase the use of natural resources.
4. Increase developmental techniques.
5. Proper management of farm.
6. Increase standard of living.
7. Youth development.
8. Leadership development.
9. Community development.
10. Slum and rural development.
11. Improving the community affairs.
12. Increase all round development.

Importance of Extension Education

Extension education include different new methods to educating the farmers, it respect the individuality and taking their own decision and help the extension worker:

(a) It helps to adopt new innovations.

(b) It solves the problems of rural villagers.

(c) It widen the knowledge through the extension workers.

(d) It bring new finding and latest technology to change the life style of the rural people.

Objectives of Extension Education

The objectives of extension education are expressions of the ends towards which our efforts are directed. In other words, an objective means a direction of movement. Before starting any programme, its objectives must be clearly stated, so that one knows where to go and what is to be achieved. The fundamental objective of extension education is the development of the people agricultural extension in our country is primarily concerned with the following main objectives:

(1) The dissemination of useful and practical information relating to agriculture, including improved seeds, fertilisers, implements, pesticides, improved cultural practices, dairying, poultry nutrition, etc.;

(2) The practical application of useful knowledge to farm and home;

(3) Thereby ultimately to improve all aspects of the life of the rural people within the framework of the national, economic and social policies involving the population as a whole.

Principles of Extension Education

The extension work is based upon some working principles and the knowledge of these principles is necessary for an extension worker. Some of these principles, as related to agricultural extension, are mentioned below.

1. ***Principles of Interest and Need.*** Extension work must be based on the needs and interests of the people. These needs and interests differ from individual to individual, from village to village, from block to block, and from state to state and therefore, there cannot be one programme for all people.

2. ***Principle of Cultural Difference.*** Extension work is based on the cultural background of the people with whom the work is done. Improvement can only begin from the level of the people where they are. This means that the extension worker has to know the level of the traditions, beliefs, values, etc. Before starting the extension programme.

3. ***Principle of Participation.*** Extension helps people of help themselves. Good extension work is directed towards assisting rural families to work out their own problems rather than giving them readymade solutions. Actual participation and experience of people in these programmes creates self-confidence in them and also they learn more by doing.

4. ***Principle of Adaptability.*** People differ from each other, one group differs from another group and conditions also differ from place to place. An extension programme should be flexible, so that necessary changes can be made whenever needed, to meet the varying conditions.

5. ***The Grassroots Principle of Organisation.*** A group of rural people in local community should sponsor extension work. The programme should fit

in with the local conditions. The aim of organising the local group is to demonstrate the value of the new practices or programmes so that more and more people would participate.

6. ***The Leadership Principle.*** Extension work is based on the full utilisation of local leadership. The selection and training of local leaders to enable them to help to carry out extension work is essential to the success of the programme. People have more faith in local leaders and they should be used to put across a new idea so that it is accepted with the least resistance.

7. ***The Whole-Family Principle.*** Extension work will have a better chance of success if the extension workers have a whole-family approach instead of piecemeal approach or separate and integrated approach. Extension work, therefore, for the whole family, i.e., for male, female and the youth.

8. ***Principle of Co-operation.*** Extension is a co-operative venture. It is a joint democratic enterprise in which rural people co-operate with their village, block and state officials to pursue a common cause.

9. ***Principle of Satisfaction.*** The end-product of the effort of extension teaching is the satisfaction that comes to the farmer, his wife or youngsters as the result of solving a problem, meeting a need, acquiring a new skill or some other changes in behaviour. Satisfaction is the key to success in extension work. "A satisfied customer is the best advertisement."

10. ***The Evaluation Principle.*** Extension is based upon the methods of science, and it needs constant evaluation. The effectiveness of the work is

measured in terms of the changes brought about in the knowledge, skill, attitude and adoption behaviour of the people.

Philosophy of Extension Education

Philosophy play vital role in deciding the pros and cons on the life of an individual. Extension philosophy based on the hypothesis that rural people are very intelligent, are very sincere to adopt new informations, very keen desired to utilise this information for their individual and the society. Different philosophy play vital role in welfare programme for community. The basic philosophy of extension education is provide change for rural people, educate then, enhance their better standard of living, secure the community, social welfare programme, widen the knowledge of rural people, educational support, provide new technique to educate then by extension worker.

Community Development

Community development programme was defined as a technique by which people's effort are combined with governmental authorities to improve the economic, cultural social condition of communities, to integrate. These communities into the life of the nation and to enable them to contribute fully to rational progress. Community development programme include community strive for self improvement, use of government assistance and need people's participation. It is a process of social and economical progress for community.

Community development was secure development of material and resources in rural areas and realise the standard of living of the reveal community.

Objectives of community development are:

(a) Area development with all round progress.

(b) Self help programme.

(c) Development of the whole community with special emphasis on weaker section.

Community Development (Now Rural Development) and Extension Service in India

The community development programme in India aiming at the all-round development of the rural people and the Extension Service as a nationwide organisation achieve set up of Extension Service is the outcome of several years efforts and reforms made over the years. The evolution of this programme and the new set up are described in four stages:

Stage I—Pre-Independence Era (1866-1947)

Stage II—Post-Independence Era (1947-1953)

Stage III—Community Development and National Extension Service Era (1953-1960)

Stage IV—Intensive Agricultural Development Era (1960 onwards)

Stage I. Pre-Independence Era (1866-1947)

During the pre-independence era, various scattered and shortlived efforts were made towards rural development in various parts of the country by individuals or some organisations. Notable among these were Mahatma Gandhi's work at Sevagram. Tagore's work at Shantiniketan Spencer Hatch's efforts at Marthandam, F.L. Brayne's work at Gurgaon, Firka Development Scheme in Tamil Nadu, India Village Service, etc. It was during this period that the Department of Agriculture came into being in June 1871 under the then Government of India, and by 1882 agricultural departments in most of the provinces started functioning in skeleton form. Recognising the need for new and improved methods of cultivation based on agricultural research, the then government of India also set up an Institute of Agricultural Research at Pusa in Bihar in 1905. Though valuable work was done there and useful information was obtained as a result of agricultural research, and attempts were made from time to time to carry the results of investigations to the farmer's field, the progress was very slow. The bulk of new agricultural knowledge and skill remained unknown to tillers of the soil because of the lack of effective and adequate extension service. The villages continued to remain neglected and disorganized. The yield of crops were low, the animals remained underfed with very low productivity. The villager's lot, on the whole, presented a gloomy picture.

In fact, a number of reforms took place in India during this period. In order to avoid the recurrence of famines, Famine Commissions were appointed from time to time and they made very valuable recommendations. But it was the Royal Commission on Agriculture's Recommendation (1928) which established a firm foundation for co-ordinated research and effective agricultural administration. As a result, the Imperial Council of Agricultural Research (now Indian Council of Agricultural Research) was established in 1929. The main recommendations of this Commission were:

(1) Full measures of success cannot be achieved unless the organisation is based on research interchange should be freely permitted between the administrative and research and teaching branches in the years of service. Promotions to research posts in the superior provincial agricultural services from provincial agricultural services should be permitted to cases of outstanding merit;

(2) There should be a body for agricultural research at the national legal for promotion, guidance and co-ordination of agricultural research work in India. It will also take up training of research workers, impart information to agricultural and veterinary workers and arrange for the publication of scientific papers;

(3) The director of agriculture should have in him a combination of an administrative capacity and high scientific qualifications; and

(4) The field recruitment to the superior provincial agricultural services in any province should not be restricted to the province itself or to India.

Besides the agricultural departments, there were other development departments, such as health education, irrigation and animal husbandry, but all these departments were working in isolation and reaching the people directly, without any co-ordination among themselves.

Stage II. Post-Independence Era (1947-1953)

Grow-More-Food Campaign. The urgent need for stepping up food production was realised even in the pre-Independence era and a Grow-More-Food Campaign was started Under the campaign, targets for increased agricultural production were laid down for the first time on an all India basis.

But the campaign failed to achieve its targets. Soon after Independence (1947), the Central Government redefined the objectives of the Grow-More-Food Campaign as the attainment of self-sufficiency in foodgrains by 1952, and simultaneously increased the targets of production of other crops to meet the shortfall as a result of the partition of the country. At the same time arrangements were made for integration and co-ordination of the entire campaign for increasing agricultural production. Some state governments associated the public with working of the campaign by setting up non-official committees at the village, teluka, district and state levels. The plans were revised from time to time to make the campaign more effective.

Grow-More-Food Enquiry Committee Report. Though efforts were made to revitalize the Grow-More-Food Campaign, it was observed that the system was not functioning properly and the cultivator's response to the programme was very poor. As a result Government of India in 1952 appointed a committee known as the GMF Enquiry Committee to example the working of the Grow-More-Food Campaign.

The findings of this committee revealed that the problem of food production was much wider than the mere elimination of food imports and that agricultural improvement was a very important part of a much wider problem of raising the level of rural life in the country. The committee came to the conclusion that it was only by bringing about an appreciable improvement in the standards of rural life to make it fuller and richer that the rural masses could be awakened to take interest in not only increasing agricultural production but also improving their own conditions and creating a will to live better. The committee also pointed out that (i) all aspects of village life were interrelated, (iii) improvement could be brought about by a number of detached programmes operating, independently, (iii) there was lack of unity of efforts, (iv) the available finances was not adequate, and (v) the rural community as a whole did not participate effectively in the campaign. In short, "the movement did not arouse nationwide enthusiasm and did not become a mass movement for raising the level of village life."

In its recommendations, the Committee proposed the formation of development block, each consisting of 100 to 120 villages, and the appointment of revenue officers as development officers or extension officers assisted by technical officers for agriculture animal husbandry co-ordination and engineering. For actual work in villages, the Committee suggested the appointment of one village level worker for every five or ten villages. "He will be the joint agent for all development activities and will convey to the farmer, the lessons of research, and to experts the problems of the farmers, and arrange supplies and services needed by the farmers, including preliminary assistance in the animal and plant disease." The committee also described broadly the functions of the extension service, the manner in which the extension organisation, would operate, the arrangements required in training of the required staff, the way in which non-official leadership should be associated with the work of village development at the village taluka district and state levels. The need for setting up an independent organisation of the suggestions made the manner in which the assistance should rendered to the state governments as well as to villagers for development work, the role of the central and stage governments in this effort was also emphasized by the committee.

Based on these recommendations, the Planning Commission, which was set up earlier by the government of India to prepare a plan for development consistent with the available resources, gave the highest priority to the development of agriculture and irrigation in the First Five-Year Plan. The Commission fixed substantially high targets of internal production and decided as recommended by the Enquiry Committee, that the drive for food production should form part of plans for overall agricultural development, and that agricultural improvement in its turn should form an integral part of the much wider efforts for raising the level of rural life. The commission prescribe "Community Development" as the method for initiating the process of transformation of the social and economic life of villages and "Rural Extension" as its agency.

The Etawah Pilot Project (1948-1952). The idea of intensive all-around development work in a compact area was put into practice as a Pilot Project in Rural Planning and Development in the Etawah District in Uttar Pradesh in 1948, which can be regarded as a forerunner of the Community Development Project in India. Albert Merger, an American Engineer, played the key role in the initiation and implementation of the project. The programme was based on the principle of self-help, democracy integrated approach, felt needs of the people, rigorous planning and realistic targets, institutional approach, co-operation between the extension service and the supply agencies and the collaboration by technical and social scientists. After an initial period of trial and error, a new administrative pattern was evolved. It percolated to the village level; the activities of different nation-building departments were channeled through one common agency and a multipurpose concept of village. The project was supervised by a district planning officer assisted by four specialist officers and other supporting staff.

The Community Development Project (1952). As a result of the Grow-More-Food Enquiry Committee Report and the successful experience of the Etawah Project, 15 Pilot Projects were started in 1952 in selected states with the financial assistance received from the Ford Foundation. Besides helping to increase agriculture production and bettering the overall economic condition of the farmers, these projects were want to serve as a training ground for the extension personnel. It was soon realised that for the creation of an urge among the rural population to live a better life and to achieve permanent plentitude and economic freedom in the villages, a much bolder and dynamic effort was called for. It was recognized that the success of this new effort depended upon and whole hearted co-operation of the beneficiaries, government officials and non-officials at every stage, the education of rural masses in the technique of rural development and the timely provision of adequate supplies of the needed inputs and other requirements.

For undertaking this new programme, the Government of India entered into an operational agreement with the Government of the USA under the Technical Co-operation Programme Agreement. Under this Agreement, 55 Community Development Projects were started in different parts of the country on 2 October 1952 for three years.

The projects covered nearly 25,260 villages and a population of 6.4 millions. Each project in turn consisted of about 300 villages covering 400-500 square miles and having a population of about two lakhs. The project area was divided into three development blocks, each comprising 100 villages and a population 60,000 to 70,000. The development blocks, in turn were divided into groups of 5-10 villages, each group being in the charge of a multipurpose village-level worker. The main aims of these projects were: to increase agricultural production by all possible means to tackle the problems of unemployment to improve village communication, to foster primary education, public health and recreations, to improve housing, to promote indigenous handicrafts and small-scale industries and to improve the villager's lot through their own primary effort. In short, the programme aimed at achieving all-round socio-economic transformation of the rural people.

Stage III. Community Development and National Extension Service Era (1953-1960)

In view of a very enthusiastic response received from the rural population in all projects and the keenness shown and the demand made by the people for Community Development Programmes the Government of India decided to extend it rapidly to other parts of the country. However, owing to limited financial and technical manpower resources, it was also decided to launch along with Community Development Projects, a programme which was somewhat less comprehensive and to integrate both under one comprehensive service, the National Extension Service was inaugurated on 2nd October 1953. Whereas under the Community Development Projects intensive development work was taken up in all fields, the scheme of National Extension Service was designed to provide the essential basic staff and a small fund for the people to start the development work essentially on the basis of self-help. The operational unit of this service was a N.E.S. Block comprising about 100 villages and 60,000 to 70,000 people. The N.E.S. Blocks were later converted into Community Development Blocks which had higher budget provisions in order to take up more intensive development programmes. The Pattern of Community Development Programme was further revised (modified with effect from 1 April 1958). According to this pattern, there were four stages:

(1) Pre-Extension Stage, (2) Stage 1 Blocks, (3) Stage II Blocks, and (4) Post-Stage II Blocks.

(1) ***Pre-Extension Stage.*** At this stage there was a budget provision of Rs. 18,800 for one year The staff consisted of a block development officer, one agricultural extension officer and five village-level workers whose main duties were to survey the whole block area to prepare the ground work for the intensive stage and conduct agricultural demonstrations.

(2) ***Stage I Blocks.*** After one year of the Pre-Extension stage, the block stepped into Stage with a budget provision of Rs. 12 lakh for five years for intensive development. During this period, provision was made to have one block development officer, eight extension officers, ten village level workers (VLWs), two gram sevikas, three stockmen (veterinary) one physician and 3-4 midwives, one compounder, a sanitary inspector and the necessary office staff. It was generally expected that because of intensive work during this period the programme would gain momentum and the people would subsequently follow up the programme of their own accord.

(3) ***Stage II Blocks.*** In this stage the staffing pattern was more or less the same but there was a difference in the budget provision. The budget in this stage was five lakh of rupees for a period of five years, i.e. one lakh per year.

(4) ***Post-stage II Blocks.*** This was the permanent stage. It was meant for the follow up work. The budget was one lakh of rupees per year. At this stage, all the development activities as in Stage II,

under the various heads, such as agriculture, animal husbandry and co-operation, were to continue.

Starting with 55 Community Development Projects in 1952, the entire country was covered with the Community Development Programme by 1963. In all, there are 5,263 blocks, besides 101 tribal development blocks, a block is the unit of planning and development. This is a new administrative unit meant foe tackling the problems of the rural people in entirety and in a concerted and co-ordinated manner.

In this new set up of Community Development Blocks all the Nation-building government departments were brought together and in order to ensure co-ordination at the block level, a new post of a block development officer was created. This officer is the co-ordinator of the programme and team leader and is supported by 8 extension officers drawn from the development departments. They were one each from the fields of agriculture, animal husbandry, co-operative panchayat, rural industry, rural development, social education and welfare of women and children. Each normal block was provided with 10 village level workers and two gram sevikas (lady VLWs).

Under this new set up, the block is treated as an administrative unit for all the development departments, and the village-level work is the contact person between these departments and the people.

Panchayati Raj System. After the initiation of the Community Development and National Extension Service in India and its working for sometime, it was realized that the people's participation was not coming forth to the desired extent.

The objectives of a planned development programme, such as the Community Development Programme, could be achieved only if the later energies of the people were released to revive the village communities, so that local leadership might develop and enable the local people to take up the planning and implementation of development programme themselves. In order to achieve this objective, it was decided in 1958 to introduce the Panchayati Raj as recommended by the Balwant Rai Mehta Committee. This system envisages a three-tier system at the district block and village level, as indicated below:

District level—Zila Parishad

Block—Panchayat Samiti

Village Level—Village Panchayat

The Panchayati Raj system emphasized the importance of planning from below, so that the needs and aspirations of the local people may be viewed in the context of the local resources and what the government can provide.

According to this system a Panchayat will be established in each village. These village Panchayats would be responsible for the planning and implementation of the Community Development and Extension Programmes at the village level. At the block level the Panchayat Samities consisting of all the presidents of the village Panchayats in the block and some co-opted members are constituted. The Panchayat Samiti is in complete charge of the planning and implementation of the Community Development Programmes. The B.D.O. is the chief executive officer of the Samiti and all the extension officers are subordinate to him. The President of the Samiti is in charge of the administration of the entire staff and of the programme as approved by the Samiti. The financial resources of the Samiti consist of money derived from land revenues taxes, funds allotted for Community development, funds received from All-India Boards, etc., contributions from Panchayats and the people.

The third tier of the Panchayati Raj is the Zila Parishad consisting of all the presidents of the Panchayat Samitis in the district, the people's representatives such as the Members of Legislative Assemblies, Members of Parliament, and the District Collector and some co-opted members. Thee Zila Parishad consolidates plans prepared in respect of all the block in the district and co-ordinates activities of the Samities.

Organisational Set Up for Community Development Extension Service. The organisational set up for Community Development Programme runs from the national level through state district and block levels to the village level and there are three main constituents of this new set up.

(a) The direct-line staff such as State Development Commissioner, B.D.O. and Village Level Worker.

(b) The auxiliary or specialist staff, such as different heads of technical departments at the state and district levels and extension officers at the block level.

(c) Panchayati Raj System— The Zila Parishads, Block Samitis and Village Panchayats.

(a) ***National Level.*** At the National level programme, the policies are formulated by the National Development Council presided over the Prime Minister of India. Membership of the Council consists of the Central ministers of the concerned ministers, chief ministers of all states and members of the Planning Commission. The Planning Commission provides guidance for plan formulation and gives it approval to annual and Five-Year Plans of the states as well as of the Centre. The Ministry of Agriculture and Irrigation is responsible for giving national guidance, policy formulation and technical assistance in regard to Agriculture Extension and Community Development (now Rural Development Programmes). In the Agriculture department, the Agricultural Commissioner, Government of India, assisted by a number of assistant commissioners and directors, with the supporting staff, is in charge of all agricultural development programmes at the national level. Within this Department, special mention may be made of the Directorate of Extension Training responsible for the training Extension officers, VLWs, instructors of Village-Level Workers Training Centres and others and the Directorate of Farm Information which is concerned with the dissemination of new agricultural technology and innovations through various media.

(b) ***State Level.*** At state level also, there is usually a State Development Committee presided over by the Chief Minister of the state with the other concerned ministers as its members. This Committee is responsible for the state's plan and programmes and for fixing the targets for regions and districts. Besides this committee, there are usually a number of other advisory or technical committees.

As regards the actual administrative functioning, the State Development Commissioner is the top level executive responsible for directing, co-ordinating and providing overall guidance for development programmes and maintaining a two-way channel of communication between the state governments and the Central government. He co-ordinates the activities of different development departments, such as agriculture, animal husbandry, co-operation, Panchayati Raj health, education irrigation, power and electricity. The heads of these technical departments are responsible for planning and implementing the technical programmes and for providing the necessary technical guidance, manpower and support.

In the state, where the Panchayati Raj is operating, the Zila Parishads are responsible for planning, co-ordinating and consolidating the development programme in the district.

The District Collector is the key official who co-ordinates the activities of all development departments at the district level. The district-level technical heads of agriculture animal husbandry, co-operation, panchayats, public health, irrigation, education and rural industries are responsible for planning and implementing the development programmes relating to their departments. Administratively, they are responsible to the district collector on one hand and to their state heads of development departments on the other.

(c) ***District Level.*** At the district level also, there is usually a District Development of District Planning Committee presided over by the District Collector or Deputy Commissioner. The other members of this committee are the heads of the departments in the district, chairman and vice-chairman of the district boards, representatives of voluntary organisations, local bodies and members of parliament and state legislatures.

At the non-official level in the states, where the Panchayati Raj has been implemented the Panchayati Samiti (also called the Block this Samiti) has the statutory powers for formulating and executing development programmes. The Samiti is assisted by the B.D.O. and the extension officers. Wherever the Panchayati Raj is not working, there are block development advisory committees.

(d) ***Block Level.*** A district is subdivided into a number of community development programmes. The Block development officer is the head of the block team, and co-ordinates all the activities of the development departments at the block level. He is assisted by eight extension officers from different fields, namely agriculture, animal husbandry, health, co-operation, panchayats engineering, social education and rural industry.

(e) ***Village Level.*** At the village level, the multi-purpose village-level worker is the man extension staff. He is the last extension functionary in the administrative hierarchy and is the main contact person. He is responsible for all developmental work at the village level, and forms a connecting link between the various technical departments and the rural people. Usually, in a normal community development block, there are 10 village-level workers. Their number has been double in the Intensive Agricultural Development Programme (IADP) blocks.

On the non-official side, usually there is a Panchayat in every village or for a cluster of villages and is responsible for planning and implementing the community development programmes and ensuring people's participation in them.

Agricultural Universities. While the various administrative set-ups, as described earlier were tried and adopted, another notable innovation for improving the standard and quality of agricultural education, research and field extension (extension education) was introduced in India in the form of agricultural universities in various states. The first such university established in 1960 was the Govind Ballabh Pant University of Agricultural Science and Technology at Pantnagar (Uttar Pradesh). Subsequently, in each state one (in some states more than one) agricultural university was established and at present there are twenty-two such Universities in India. In these Universities, teaching, research and extension education are integrated. For extension education programmes and activities, each of these Universities has a directorate of extension education, headed by a director who is supported by a team of subject matter specialists from all the major disciplines, such as genetics, agronomy, animal husbandry soil science entomology, plant pathology, horticulture, agricultural economics, agricultural engineering and extension education. The directorate of extension education of the university is primarily responsible for keeping the extension personnel of the states department of agriculture up to date with the new agricultural technology, communication of new agricultural technology to farmers, the training to farmers and extension personnel bringing out suitable extension literature for use by the farmers and extension workers and carrying out extension-education programme and developmental active

Stage IV. Intensive Agricultural Development Era (1960 Onwards)

Intensive Agricultural District Programme (Package Programme). Under the Community Development Programme, the production efforts and the available resources were diffused over the entire country. The educational and extension efforts among the millions of farmers to be tackled remained thin and restricted. By the middle of the Third Five-Year Plan, it became increasingly evident that agricultural development was not making satisfactory progress. As a result of the report of the Ford Foundation team, known as "India's Food Crisis and Steps of Meet." It a significant departure took place during the period and a new programme known as the "Intensive Agricultural District Programme", based on the principles of concentration and better management of resources and efforts in potential and responsive areas, with assured water supply, was started in 1960. Since then, at least one district in each state has been covered under this programme. The scheme not only involves the adoption of a package of new practices, but also ensures the availability of credit and production inputs, adequate research information training and education of farmers and extension personnel, storage and marketing arrangements and price assurance which would encourage the farmers to adopt scientific methods of farming. Each intensive Agricultural District Programme district is the charge of the project officer who is assisted by an assistant project officer, four or five subject-matter specialists and other supporting staff. At the block level, besides a block development officer, there are four agricultural extension officers, two co-operative extension officers and a few officials from other fields. The number of VLWs is 20 in each block. A little later a similar programme, but less in intensity and thinner in staffing pattern, was started in 1964. This programme is known as the "Intensive Agricultural Area Programme (IAAP)." Now about 10 per cent of the total cultivated area in the country is under the Intensive Agricultural District Programme and Intensive Agricultural Area Programme.

High-yielding Varieties Programme. A new dimension which was created in the community development programme has been the Agricultural Production Programme, known as the High-Yielding Varieties Programme of wheat and paddy and hybrids of maize, sorghum and bajra evolved and introduced in the country since 1965-1966. To start with, 100 districts were selected for this purpose, but later on it spread to other areas also. This programme aimed at covering 13,162 hectares by 1970-1971. This significant development has a vital bearing on the increasing of agricultural production and the bumper harvest of over 108 million tonnes of good grains during 1970-1971 has clearly shown the impact of this new strategy.

Multiple-Cropping Programme. Yet another strategy recently introduced in the country is of multiple-croping which aims at maximising production per unit of land and per unit of time by taking three or four crops from the same piece of land in a year. This has been made possible because of the new short-duration, high-yielding varieties and improved agricultural technology.

Small Farmer's Development Agency (SFDA). The aims of the SFDA are to identify the problems of the small farmers, to prepare appropriate programmes to overcome them and ensure the availability of inputs and credit. In all, about 50 SFDA projects have been established throughout the country under the Fourth Five-Year Plan and Rs. 68 crore were allotted for these projects during the Fourth Plan.

Marginal Farmers and Agricultural Labourers Projects. The principle objective of this scheme is to assist the marginal cultivators in making the maximum productive use of their small holdings by undertaking horticulture, animal husbandry and dairying. Efforts are also to be directed towards bringing in larger incomes by channelling credits, improved inputs and improved practices. Under this scheme, 41 projects were scheduled to be established throughout the country in the Fourth Five-Year Plan to cover farmers having holdings of not more than one hectare and agricultural labourers having a homestead and earning half or more of their income from agricultural wages. Each Project aimed at covering about 20,000 households during the Fourth Five-Year Plan, of which about two-thirds would be from the marginal farmers and the rest from agricultural labourers.

The Integrated Area Development Programme. The foregoing review clearly indicates that most of the programmes for agricultural development have lacked a totality of approach and have been concerned with one or only a few aspects of a given agricultural situation. A recent thinking therefore, has been going on in the country for sometime and some states and agricultural universities have already taken initiative for the "Integrated Area Development in Agriculture", which implies planning for given geographic area with respect to all aspects of agricultural development, with a more comprehensive approach, built around ***Krishi Vigyan Kendras*** and generating viable rural communities.

Education and Training for Implementing Agricultural Strategy. The acceptance of a progressive democratic approach based upon science and technology implied that the extension workers and the farmers in the whole process of change would work as equal partners. The training of extension workers as well as of farmers was, therefore, emphasized from the very beginning of this programme and a number of special kinds of institutions, including ***gram sevaks*** and ***gram sevikas*** training centres, orientation and study training centres, extension wings in the college of agriculture veterinary and home science, extension educational institutes, national institute or community development Panchayati Raj training centres, etc. were started in the country. The principles and concepts of selective areas pattern and intensive agriculture pattern threw a new challenge and an integrated training programme for the farmers farm women and young farmers has recently been initiated through the country through farmer's training centres. The agricultural universities and research institutes are also playing a very important role in organising and conducting training programmes for farmers and extension workers.

Extension Education System

Extension education system includes in extension educational programmes. These approaches are grouped in four categories:-

1. The extension approach.
2. The training approach.
3. The cooperative self-help approach.
4. The integrated development approach.

1. ***Extension Approach.*** The extension approaches uses the extension teaching methods for educating the people. It believes that rural services can transforms static economy into dynamic economy. When improving the status of family and society life, it emphasises the communication of information about innovative technical practices. It is mostly followed in America and Asia today and is referred to as the conventional or classical model of extension. This model was prepared by the professors of the land grant colleges who sought to make agricultural extension a separate scientific profession with its basic concepts, theory, principles and methodologies.

Objectives

(a) To persuade and help farmers, improving the production level.

(b) Adopting improved agricultural practices

(c) Improving the rural family life.

(d) Educating the women, youth in rural and slum areas.

Organisation. The extension service is mostly under the ministry of rural development or department of agriculture. It operates within the broad framework of national rural policies, aims and objectives. It is a network structure of trained field worker at the base supervised and guided by more highly qualified administrators and specialists at village, block, district, division, provincial and national levels. The extension service relies on the agricultural universities for the basic rice preparation of its personnel and for technical messages on research organisations of the ministry of agriculture and agricultural universities.

Work

(1) Transfer of production technologies.

(2) Farm planning and management.

(3) Use of credit and marketing of produce.

(4) Relayed the technical messages through experts to farmers.

(5) Adoption of desirable innovations.

(6) Awareness among the farmers.

2. ***Training Approach.*** Extension approach include the training approach which has different basic educational tradition and philosophy related to institutionalised schooling. Training approaches emphasises on more systematic and deeper learning of specific basic skills and knowledge. Training programmes involve assembling the learners in a training centre for a sustained period of instruction. These trained extension workers are supposed to transmit the useful knowledge gained by them to the rural people. It is based on the assumption that outsiders (extension workers) within superior knowledge and wisdom can help in solving the problems of rural society and visit system is a good example of the training approach. This approach is based on the

assumption that there is a gap between average productivity of various crops on the farmer's fields and the potential. This gap can be minimised by intensive extension efforts, The training and visit system evolved by Benor is being used in most of the developing countries with assistance from the world bank to reduce this gap.

Objectives

(1) Increase the crop productivity at maximum level.

(2) It provide knowledge to farmers to utilise their own land.

(3) It provide technique to increase crop growth.

(4) It widen the knowledge of farmers to adopt new agricultural practices.

Organisation. Extension service is mostly under the department of agriculture. The trained persons are pasted at each level starting from the village to the national level. The framing to the staff at the lower level is given by the subject matter specialists of the agricultural university and the department of agriculture. The messages or impact points for each crop are prepared in coordination with the agricultural university specialists and the staff of the departments of agriculture. These impact points are emphasised in the weekly and fortnightly training sessions. The staff than undertakes a visit programme for the transfer of knowledge now to the farmers.

Work

(1) Training the staff of the department of agriculture.

(2) Technical messages relayed to the farmers.

(3) Spread the messages with the help of farmers.

(4) Give emphasis on farmer guidance.

(5) Adopting new technology.

3. ***Cooperative Self-help Approach.*** It starts with the assumption that the complex process of rural transformation must begin with changes in the rural people themselves. This change may be in their attitudes towards change, in their aspirations for improvement and in their perceptions of themselves. They should realise their own inherent power, individually and collectively, to better their conditions. Building of local institutions for cooperative self-help and governance is the vital element of this approach.

Objectives

1. Villagers decide their own representative to represent their needs.
2. Organic themselves.
3. Registered their society and choose a chairman.
4. Hold daily, weekly and monthly meeting and taking full attendance.
5. Select a person and trained him for organiser.
6. Keep proper records.
7. Supervised production credit.
8. Adopt latest agriculture techniques.
9. Regular savings.
10. Make an association.
11. Hold regular teaching classes.
12. Members training programmes.

Organisation. For agricultural education and rural education, village cooperate play vital role, as a prime agency. The organiser becomes the key agricultural teacher in his own community, rather than the outside extension worker. Representatives came for regular training to their academy and received expert advice and assistance an problems identified through discussion in village. The village cooperative society become more organised and more complex. The duty of organiser and formers mere combined in a cooperative manager who was paid on an incentive basis.

Work

(i) It provide skill training for particular needs.

(ii) It provide district training for planning, development and coordination for local programmes.

(iii) It provide Personnel Academy Adviser.

(iv) It provide educational material supporting the programme.

4. ***Integrated Development Approach.*** Integrated development approach emphasises the need of coordinating different agencies under a single management system of essential component required to get agricultural or rural development moving. The management system may be highly authoritarian, credit may be designed to provide an important role for local people in planning, decision making and implementation of the programmes. The main emphasis is an rational development and coordination of all principal factors required for rural and agricultural development. India could not achieve desired impact in agricultural production in community development programme. Intensive agricultural district programme was launched in particular district and develop approaches to solve the problem of rural development to solve the problem of rural development.

Objectives

1. Adequate farm credit through strengthened cooperatives.
2. Adequate supplies of fertilisers, pesticides, improved seeds, and other essential production needs through services.
3. Participating farmers through assured price agreements for cereals.
4. Marketing arrangements.
5. Educational, technical and farm management.
6. Participation of farmers for increase production.
7. Farm planning and village planning.
8. Public mark programme.
9. Evaluation of the programme.
10. Increase resources for maximum level.

Organisation. In first staff particular effective districts were selected for IADP. Each districts had a director, team of agricultural experts, and chief civil administration. The experts had plan to implement agricultural programme because the particular district accorded with a special fertiliser, supplies of mater, soil condition etc.

Work

1. Give special attention to particular district.
2. Instruct to increase efforts to agriculture.
3. Provide useful analytical structure for the sample.

Early Efforts in Rural Reconstruction

1. ***Gurgaon Attempt.*** This was organised by F.L. Bryne, Collector of Gurgaon in Haryana NCR of Delhi in 1920. He was prompted by the poverty and misery of the people. He emphasis on this project was increasing farm production, decrease the expenses an social, cultural and religious functions, improving health. Standards and organising welfare programmes village representative were selected for who conduct folk songs, use of films, drama etc. to approach the villagers. Due to some defect the project cannot bot developed and villager cannot participate in the programme which planned for then.

2. ***Sevagram Attempt.*** It was started under the guidance of Mahatma Gandhi in 1920. Very high personnel standards were set in the project which were difficult for common man to reach, so the project could no provide the result.

Objective

(a) To provide service to underprivileged people.

(b) Achieving self dependency.

(c) Provide basic education for rural people.

(d) Establish training centres.

(e) Removal of untouchability.

(f) Stressing on women's education.

3. ***ACRSE Attempt.*** The American Council on Rural Special Education is an organisation comprised of special educators, general educators, related service providers, administrators, teacher trainers, researchers, and parents who are committed to the enhancement of services to students and individuals living in rural areas. It was found in 1981,

by a group of individuals interested in unique challenges of rural people who need special services.

Objectives

(a) To promote the growth and development of each member of minorities.

(b) To promote cultural diversity and empowerment of minorities.

(c) To faster quality education.

(d) To improving education for disabled.

(e) To promote collaborative partnership with rural organisation.

4. ***Shriniketan Attempt.*** This project was established in 1921 in Bengal by Rabindranath Tagore and Elmhirst. This project cannot make much headway due to lack of funds, financial support, less educative staff, urbanisation and centralisation.

Objectives

(a) win the friendship of villagers.

(b) Make honest effort to assist them.

(c) Solving their pressing problems.

(d) Teach the villagers with better methods for growing crops.

(e) Encourage villagers to learn about art and craft.

(f) To provide mutual aids.

5. ***Martadum Attempt.*** This project was started by Hatch in Travancore state in 1921 under the auspices of the

Y.M.C.A. This project was stopped due to lack of funds, government help and religious bias of the institution.

Objectives

(a) Bringing a complete upward development for rural people.

(b) Self help with expert guidance.

(c) Trained villagers to improve their performance.

(d) Making people conscious for their needs.

(e) Organising reconstruction programme to include the poorest.

6. ***Etawah Attempt.*** This project was established by the American architect Albert Mayer in 1948. The demonstration process was used to convey New ideas. The project to be successful and on a similar pattern, extension organisation was organised in India.

Objectives

(a) Improvement in production.

(b) Social improvement and self-reliance.

(c) Trained the villagers.

(d) Cooperate the agencies.

2

Extension Educational Psychology

Concepts of Extension Educational Psychology

1. ***Instincts.*** It is complex inherited quality to all members of a species compelling each individual.

(a) To perceive and pay attention to contain situation.

(b) To experience positive or negative emotional excitement on perceiving then.

(c) To act in a way which is likely in the long run to preserve the individual.

The common instincts are parental, gregariousness sex, self assertion, escape, acquisition, etc. These intimates are observable in human being.

2. ***Drive.*** Drive means need. These two terms are closely related; need refers to a condition of lack or deficiency in organisation. Drive is defined as tendency initiated by shifts in the physiological balance in the body. The individual is restless because of drive. Thus drives are the sources of energy.

3. ***Motive.*** Motive is that which moves are activates. It refers to same internal activation within individual. Motives

are the directing tendencies inside the individual follow a particular course of action motives are goal directed. Motivator is energy mobilisation towards the attainment of goal. Students are not interested in learning without motivation.

4. ***Attitude.*** Attitude is the degree of positive or negative feelings associated with some psychological objects towards which people differ in varying degrees.

In develops in 3 phases:

(a) Towards the object.

(b) The effect connected with the object.

(c) The action that can be undertaken with respect to that object.

Attitude are not innate but are formed as a result of the individual contact with object. Attitude affects individual course of action. The change of attitude may lead to action.

5. ***Intelligence.*** Individual differ in their ability to learn, to adjust to new situation, manage things, persons and ideas. Intelligence is defined as the capacity of solving problems by using past experiences, adjusting with new things and understanding abstract things by using symbols.

Mental age was related with chronological age to obtain the intelligence quotient of the individual.

$$IQ = \frac{\text{Mental Age}}{\text{Chronological Age}} \times 100$$

$$IQ = \frac{\text{M.A.}}{\text{C.A.}} \times 100$$

6. ***Culture.*** It is defined as the socially standardised ways of feeling thinking and acting which an individual acquires as a member of the society. Man is not born with

culture but he learns it through parents, friends and social institutions. Culture shared by its members, Culture provides specific ways of satisfying the physical and social needs of the individual.

7. ***Socialisation.*** It is a process of inducting the individual into the social and cultural world to play his role as a member of society. The process of socialisation starts from the birth to continue till death.

The personality of person energies out this process of socialisation.

8. ***Personality.*** Personality is dynamic organisation within the individual of the psychological systems that determine the unique adjustments to his environment. Personality is not static, which is continuously changing and growing, Personality is which an individual starts his life but it is what he acquires and develops in the course of life and experiences. It includes psychological system.

Classification of personality are based an emotional trends, physical and psychological structure and social relationship.

Steps in Extension Teaching

The teacher plans and arranges situations and activities where they learned. In effective teaching there are six steps:

1. ***Attention.*** Fareness are not always of the improvements they can make as the result of scientific research and successful experience of the other farmers. The individual attention has been focused on the change that is considered desirable, there is no recognition of a problem to be solved or a want to be satisfied. Attention is the starting point to the arousing of interest.

2. ***Interest.*** The teacher reveals to the learners that the new skill or practice will contribute to the learners welfare. The teacher should present the message alternatively and in a manner that requires little mental effort on the part of the learner. The presenting of one idea at a time, which is definitive and specific is an important factors in building interest.

3. ***Desire.*** Learners interest in new idea becomes a desire motion force sufficiently strong to compel act. The teacher convinces the learner that the information applies directly to the learner's situation. Acting on the information will satisfy the learner's need or want.

4. ***Conviction.*** The teacher knows if that the learner knows what action is necessary and just now to take that action. He also make sure that the learner visualises the action in terms of his own peculiar situation, and has acquired confidence in his own ability to do the thing.

5. ***Action.*** Unless conviction is converted into action the teaching efforts are useless. It is the job if the teacher to make it easy for the learner to act. The blocks and annoyances that might prevent action should be anticipated by the teacher and appropriate steps taken to remove or bypass them.

6. ***Satisfaction.*** Satisfaction that cames to the learner, as a result of solving problem, meeting a need acquiring a new skill or some other change in behaviour. The satisfaction and confidence resulting from the successful completion of each small job will then lead logically to the accomplishment of the difficult jobs, A satisfied customer is the best advertisement applies to extension worker as well as to the retail merchant.

Various teaching methods are not equally suited to advance each of the different steps in teaching, each method under certain circumstances makes a contribution to each step. It depends on the teacher now he, handles the situation.

Principles of Learning

1. Learning is growth likes and continued.
2. Learning should be meaningful.
3. Learning uses maximum senses.
4. Learning should be challenging and satisfying.
5. Learning should develop functional understanding of learners.
6. Learning is affected by physical and social environment.
7. Learning ability varies widely among individuals.
8. Learning is a gradual process usually requiring several exposures before change is noticed.
9. The adult have learning capacity.
10. Learning is an active process on the part of the learner.
11. Learning requires effective communication.
12. Theory and practice should be related in learning.

Learning Situation

Extension teaching is a process of creating situations that are conductive to effective learning and learning is a process through which changes in behaviour are achieved. In extension education learning of the rural people will be effective if a people learning situation is arranged and effective learning experiences are provided. This will help in achieving the objectives of extension education.

Learning is an active and international process on the part of the farmer. It taken place through experiences and therefore the extension worker should organise effective learning situations in which the rural people can have good learning experiences. These experiences may be through mental on physical action.

The good learning situation has following five elements:

1. A skillful extension worker.
2. Farmers who want and need to learn.
3. Subjects in line with the needs and abilities of the learners or farmers.
4. Teaching equipment and materials adequate for the farmers.
5. Satisfactory physical arrangements.

The extension worker should skillfully maintain the elements of the learning situation and provide satisfactory learning experiences to the people. The farmer is a centre of the learning situation and the other four element act on it. The main aim of extension education is to alter the behaviour of the farmers and the other elements are supported to help this process. The success of the learning situation should be judged from the desirable atmosphere it has created for effective learning. Extension worker must speak clearly so that the farmers can understand him. He must know the level of the farmers in terms of their knowledge of subject matter, level of education, interest in the subject matter, need for the subject matter and opportunities to apply what is learned.

The extension workers should try to reduce the bad effects on learning and help in creating a favourable situation so that the farmers can devote more time and energy in learning. By doing this he would help in achieving the objectives of extension education effectively.

Factors Effecting Adult Learning

These are the factors which influence the learning of the adults.

1. ***Age.*** The stage of adulthood means maturity, the decline of interest in recreation and increase in use of leisure. Interest are decreases with increases of age.

2. ***Environment.*** An adult in a bad environment, will not have access to some resources form his environment and this way restrict his behaviour.

3. ***Political Condition.*** Political policies affect the behaviour of the adult. It also affect the life style.

4. ***Lack of Leisure.*** Except from learning there are more urgent need which take-up an adult's time. The extension worker may also try to devise to reduce the daudgery of the people and enable than to snatch more leisure by reducing the time which must be spent on their more urgent needs.

5. ***Misuse of Leisure.*** Lack of ambition the adults fail to make use his leisure. The extension worker educate the people to utilise their time more faith-fully.

6. ***Lack of Mental Peace.*** A clean social atmosphere is essential for extension education in which an adult is tolerably free from mental worries.

7. ***Lack of Physical Comfort.*** In old age noises irritable adults so the classroom should be quiet place for then because it free from bad odours.

8. ***Lack of Meaning.*** Adult learning should be meaningful, it show the connection between the subject matter and life.

9. ***Boredom.*** In old age people are easily bored, so recreational learning should be beneficient for them to utilise the boredom.

So it is necessary to, provide adult base education for improvement their learning.

Educational Psychology

Educational psychology is empirical foundation of education. It consist of those aspects of education which can be observed, tested, and experimentally verified and as such educational psychology is the scientific foundation of education. But effectiveness of educational psychology is proved only when its methods and findings become a part of educational practices when the teachers apply.

Educational psychology as a scientific study of the life stages in the development of an individual from the time he is born until he becomes an adult.

Educational psychology is that branch of psychology which deals with teaching and learning.

Educational psychology is the study of those facts and principles of psychology which helps to explain and improve the process of education. Educational psychology thus is the body of scientific knowledge about two activities—Education and Psychology.

Nature of Educational Psychology

Educational psychology is a major branch of applied a psychology. It usually deals with human behaviour in educational situation. Education is a social process. Educational psychology gives importance on the study of topics like growth and development, learning process, intellectual, emotional and social influences etc.

Educational psychology deals with the behaviour of the learner in educational situation only. Educational psychology should limit itself within the four walls of the teaching learning process and educational environment. Following are the important factors of educational psychology:

1. The learner.
2. The learning experience.
3. The learning process.
4. The learning situation.
5. The teacher.

Therefore, the boundaries of educational psychology must be left free for future expansion so as to facilitate the inclusion of all what is created in this fixed in this field in future to solve the problems of education.

Adult Education

In extension education change are more concerned with adult or aged people. There is a lot of difference in the behaviour between adult and child. The age of adult developed than the child and more sensitive to social atmosphere. The social freedom for adult is greater than the child. A child learns ten per cent of his potentialities in the average school and completes ninety per cent of his education throughout his life.

An adult is more sensitive to success and failure then a child. He is concerned with the acquisition of mastery over something or is more power hungry. Therefore advisable to allow him occasional experience which will give him glow of success. It is necessary to point out to him the progress that he has made.

Occupation is so vital part of this scale. Extension worker should consider his occupation and acquire entry into his mental world through his occupation. Adult pick up things easily if he sees their relationship to his occupation.

If he is convinced that he will be able to earn more for himself and his family with the men learning then he will try to learn quickly. This learning related to his vocational interest will be more realistic and long lasting. An adult has a greater sense of responsibilities than a child and therefore he should be given responsibility for his own learning.

There are stronger and more permanent sentiments in the adult than in a child. The extension worker should respect and use these sentiments. The sentiments towards his family, friend and strong desire for learning are some of the sentiments which will help to extension worker.

Teaching

Teaching is the process of arranging situations that stimulate and guide the learning activity towards the goals that specify desired changes in the behaviour of the learner. It consist of providing situation in which the important things to be learned are called to the attention of the learners, their interest developed, desired aroused and action promoted.

Factors Affect on Teaching

Teaching should be successful by the effective learning. Factors are:

1. Teaching based on the needs of the people and related to life situation and problems of the learners.

2. Natural impulse of learner should be used in training. All development and education start with basic needs and drives. The teaching material should be organised in an interesting way so that the learners take interest in learning.

3. The teacher should be ultimately tried to its practical application. If the learner given chance to try out the things learned then it develops his understanding. Good teaching helps in problem solving and making a clear impression on the minds of the learner.

4. Aids may used along with new presentation. A visual appeal is the most effective approach. A picture are model presented for a short period will produce a more vivid image than a verbal description.

5. Teacher develop pleasing personality. Teacher try to develop patience, helpfulness, clarity, farmers, a sense of humour, cheerfulness, sincerity and sympathy.

6. Physical condition should be satisfactory, comfort, proper ventilation, lighting etc. because it helps in learning.

7. The course should be organised from the standpoint of learners. Learners should know what the subject matter is and how it is going to benefit them.

Learning Experiences

Good extension teaching brings about effective learning by providing effective learning experiences to rural people. The success of extension teaching depends on the change of rural people. The result of successful teaching that a farmer can and does use freely, flexibly, and confidently in his life are clearly far superior to those which he can produce only when he is given the right due on ask right question. Teaching should be that such that the learners could use the results freely and flexibly in their lives. The information of providing learning experiences to the learner should be known to all who are engaged in educational affairs. Farmers learns new techniques by physically and mentally through learning experiences. Farmers know new ideas by critical observation, hearing and typical and error of doing work, Learning experience helps the farmers to solve problems in future.

Extension worker should arrange learning situation for farmers which will provide effectiveness for learning experiences. Curriculum are important to provide guidelines to both extensive worker and the learner. Reading books, attending the training class, hearing a lecture, observing the extension programme are some important activities in which there is the idea of providing learning experiences. These activities though important are not sufficient for learning experiences. Two students can be different in learning situation.

Many methods of providing effective learning experiences are available to the extension worker. These methods are based on research and experiences. The extension worker should know them the thoroughly before organising them into learning experiences for rural people:

1. The farmers provided a chance of learning experiences in the direction of desired changes. Learner knows the thing to be done he can acquire the skill by constant efforts. If it is desired that the farmer should learn mental skill in solve the problems, he should be provided opportunities for solving such problems.

2. As per the objectives of teaching the farmers should feel satisfied under the learning experience. For showing the problems of a balanced diet in a family it will not be enough to teach the farmers the method of better cooking of vegetables but care will taken to see that the family members feel satisfaction in eating the cooked vegetables. If the cooked vegetables is distasteful or the learning experience unsavoury to then they will discontinue that practice and learning will not take place.

3. Extension worker should be capable of providing the learning experiences. If he does not know the method he has to teach or does not know the operation of the implement which he wants his students to operate then he cannot provide these learning experiences to his students. It affects their learning to a great extent.

4. Learning experiences helps in achieving more than one objective and reality helps in achieving the long term objectives of extension education. An individual try up to solve the agricultural problems of the rural people will collect more information due to curiosity about agriculture and while doing this he will also learn many things.

5. Learning experience should be within the mental and physical capacity of the farmers. Extension worker should start from the level of the farmers. If the practical aspect in the learning experience situation is beyond the capacity of the formers than naturally the aim of teaching will not be achieved.

6. Extensive worker should provide proper learning experiences which would lead to desirable objectives, objectives of education as emphasised earlier can

only be achieved through these learning experiences. This is an important part in education, and as per the situation the extension worker should provide different learning experiences.

The objectives of extension education the learning experiences should be carefully chosen and provided to the rural people.

3

Communication of Innovation

Communication

All societies have ways of spreading information and sharing ideas. Songs, proverbs, drama, dancing, religious gatherings and village meetings are just a few of the traditional means of communication that an extension agent may find in a rural area.

There are two main reasons why these means of communication are important for extension:

- The extension agent can learn from them what people in the community are saying and thinking. An understanding of local proverbs, for example, will give the agent an insight into people's knowledge of their environment and their attitudes toward farming. Songs and dances often express deeply held feelings which an extension agent should be aware of when planning his programmes.

- The extension agent can make use of these traditional means of communication to pass on information and ideas. Many extension services now use drama, puppets and songs to convey new ideas.

Contact between different cultures is far more widespread than it used to be. New methods of communication bring societies throughout the world relatively easily into contact.

On a more local scale, roads and railways have brought many changes to rural society. Travel has been made easier and more people can visit other places and learn different ways of doing things. Traders establish shops and the goods in them may act as incentives for farmers to produce more in order to buy them. Crops can be marketed more easily and farming inputs brought into rural areas more quickly and cheaply.

Air travel has also had important effects. In Papua New Guinea, air services have enabled isolated mountain communities to market vegetables in towns and mining settlements that used to be inaccessible. The aeroplane has also helped to open up previously inaccessible areas of the Peruvian and Bolivian mountain regions. Villagers can now visit other communities and receive visitors from all over the world.

Newspapers, radio and television can also bring rural people in remote areas into contact with the outside world. People in rural communities who have radio sets or who read newspapers are usually influential and can spread their knowledge or new ideas to their neighbours. Education is another way of introducing people to the ideas, values and way of life of other societies.

Communication: The sharing of ideas and information-forms a large part of the extension agent's job. By passing on ideas, advice and information, he hopes to influence the decisions of farmers. He may also wish to encourage farmers to communicate with one another; the sharing of problems and ideas is an important stage in planning group or village activities. The agent must also be able to communicate with superior officers and research workers about the situation faced by farmers in his area.

There are many ways in which extension agents and farmers communicate. In this chapter, some general principles of communication will be looked at, and the use of mass media and audio-visual aids for communication in extension work will be discussed.

Act of Communication

Any act of communication, be it a speech at a public meeting, a written report, a radio broadcast or a question from a farmer, includes four important elements:

- the *source*, or where the information or idea comes from;
- the *message*, which is the information or idea that is communicated;
- the *channel*, which is the way the message is transmitted;
- the *receiver*, who is the person for whom the message is intended.

Any communicator must consider all four elements carefully, as they all contribute to effectiveness. In considering each of these elements, the questions that follow provide a useful checklist.

The Four Elements of Communication

Receiver

- What information does the receiver want or need?
- What information can he make use of ?

- How much does the receiver already know about the particular topic?
- What attitudes does the receiver hold concerning the topic?
- Should these attitudes be reinforced, or should an attempt be made to change them?

Channel

- What will be the most effective way of sharing the information?
- What are the characteristics of the message? Does it need a visual presentation, as when crop pests are being described? Is it necessary to show movement or detailed actions (in which case, film, video or a demonstration will be needed)? If a permanent, accurate record of detailed information is required, as in farm records or fertilizer recommendations, the information should be in written or printed form.
- What channels are available to the receivers? Do they see newspapers? Can they read? Do many of them have radios?
- What are the receiver's expectations? A senior government official, for example, is more likely to take notice of a written submission followed by a personal visit.

Message

- What should the content be? A balance must be achieved between what the receiver wants to know and what the source feels the receiver ought to know.

- What form should the message take? In other words, how can the message be put into the words, pictures or symbols that the receiver will understand and take notice of ?

Source

- Where will the information come from?
- Where should the information be seen to come from? An account of a successful cooperative in a nearby village may have much more effect if it is given by the members, through a radio programme or a visit, than by an extension agent at a public meeting.
- Has information from the source proved reliable in the past?
- How credible is the source in the eyes of the receiver?

Information often passes through several channels before it reaches a particular receiver, but it is rarely passed on in exactly the same words in which it was received. In particular, technical information is often distorted as it goes from one person to another. Extension agents should aim at being accurate sources and channels of information, and should make sure that farmers have heard and fully understood any information passed on to them. Leaflets and posters can be useful reminders of the spoken word.

Not all communication is deliberate. For example, people's behaviour, the way they speak to each other or the clothes they wear reveal much about them and their attitudes. If an extension agent is always late for meetings with farmers' groups, the members may come to the conclusion that he does not take them seriously. If he wears casual clothes when addressing a formal village meeting, villagers may say that he has no respect for them. Even if this is not so, the fact that they think it is will affect their relationship with the agent and, therefore, his effectiveness. The message that is received is not always the one that the source intends to pass.

Listening

A good communicator listens more than he speaks. An extension agent who does not listen to farmers and engage in a dialogue with them is unlikely to be very effective. There are four main reasons why a two-way exchange or dialogue is more effective than a monologue.

- Information needs can be assessed.
- Attitudes concerning the topic of the communication will emerge.
- Misunderstandings that occur during the exchange can quickly be identified and cleared up.
- Relationships of mutual respect can develop. If an agent listens, farmers will know that one agent is interested in them, and they will be more likely to pay attention to what the agent has to say.

Shared Meanings

Communication is only successful when the receiver can interpret the information that the source has put into the message. An extension agent may give what he feels is a clear and concise talk, or an artist may be satisfied that he has designed a poster that conveys over the desired message, but there is no guarantee that those for whom the talk and poster are intended will interpret the message correctly. In the Figure 1, for example, the intended message is that crops should be rotated; however, many farmers may not understand the meaning of the arrows, or the symbols that stand for the different crops.

It is important that the same meanings for the words, pictures and symbols used in communication be used by the source and the receiver. If this does not happen, various kinds of problems can arise.

The agent may understand the message, but will the farmer?

Language. Even if source and receiver speak the same language, local variations or dialects may use similar words with different meanings.

Jargon. The technical language of specialists has to be translated into words that are familiar to the receiver. Extension agents need to learn what words and phrases farmers use when talking about their farming activities.

Pictures and Symbols. Attempts to communicate through pictures and visual symbols often fail because the receiver does not recognize what they represent. Interpreting pictures is a skill which, like reading, has to be learned.

Mass Media in Extension

Mass media are those channels of communication which can expose large numbers of people to the same information at the same time. They include media which convey information by sound (radio, audio-cassettes); moving pictures (television, film, video); and print (posters, newspapers, leaflets). The attraction of mass media to extension services is the high speed and low cost with which information can be communicated to people over a wide area. Although the cost of producing and transmitting a radio programme may seem high, when that cost is divided between the millions of people who may hear the programme, it is in fact a very cheap way of providing information. The cost of an hour's radio broadcast per farmer who listens can be less than one-hundredth of the cost of an hour's contact with an extension agent.

However, mass media cannot do all the jobs of an extension agent. They cannot offer personal advice and support, teach practical skills, or answer questions immediately. Their low cost suggests that they should be used for the tasks to which they are well suited. These include the following:

- Spreading awareness of new ideas and creating interest in farming innovations.
- Giving timely warnings about possible pest and disease outbreaks, and urgent advice on what action to take.
- Multiplying the impact of extension activities. A demonstration will only be attended by a small number of farmers, but the results will reach many more if they are reported in newspapers and on the radio.
- Sharing experiences with other individuals and communities. The success of a village in establishing a local tree plantation might stimulate other villages to do the same if it is broadcast over the radio. Farmers are also often interested in hearing about the problems of other farmers and how they have overcome them.
- Answering questions, and advising on problems common to a large number of farmers.
- Reinforcing or repeating information and advice. Information heard at a meeting or passed on by an extension agent can soon be forgotten. It will be remembered more easily if it is reinforced by mass media.
- Using a variety of sources that are credible to farmers. Instead of hearing advice from the

extension agent only, through mass media farmers can be brought into contact with successful farmers from other areas, respected political figures and agricultural specialists.

Mass media communication requires specialist professional skills. Few extension agents will ever be required to produce radio programmes or to make films. However, extension agents can contribute to the successful use of mass media by providing material to media producers, in the form of newspaper stories, photographs, recorded interviews with farmers, items of information about extension activities or ideas for new extension films; and by using mass media in their extension work, for example, by distributing posters and leaflets or by encouraging farmers to listen to farm broadcasts.

Audio-visual Aids in Extension

The term audio-visual aid refers to anything that an extension agent uses to help to convey the message when communicating with farmers. The spoken word is the agent's main communication tool, but, whether the agent is speaking to a large village meeting or discussing a problem in a field with a group of farmers, its impact and effectiveness can be greatly increased by the use of suitable audio-visual aids. When selected and used properly, audio-visual aids can help in the following ways:

- The interest of the audience can be maintained if the agent varies the mode of presentation. It is difficult to concentrate for long on what someone is saying; but if the agent refers to a wall chart, or illustrates a point with some slides, his audience's attention can be maintained.

- When information is presented to more than one sense (sight and touch, for example, as well as hearing), more is taken in and it is better understood and remembered.

- Processes and concepts that are difficult to express in words alone can be explained. The procedure for applying for a loan, for example, may sound confusing, but a simple chart or diagram can make the process clearer. Again, the life cycle of a crop pest can be explained by showing a series of slides or drawings.

- The effects of decisions and actions that farmers might take can be shown. Photographs of a cattle dip or a model of a cooperative store can give farmers a clear idea of just what it is they might be considering.

- Pictures can have a more immediate impact on our emotions than words. Photographs of a heavy crop, for example, are likely to arouse interest more effectively than details of yields read out by an extension agent.

What is Innovation?

Meaning of Innovation

While many organizations acknowledge that innovation is important to their growth and success, the term "innovation" is still without a consistent, agreed to definition in the business world. So in addition to our definition, we offer some others you may find useful:

- "Innovators can hold a situation in chaos for long periods of time without having to reach a resolution...won't give up... have a long term commitment to their dream ... innovators introduce a maximum of tension into the thinking process, unifying concepts that often appear to be opposed, solving problems which appear impossible."

- Incremental innovation seeks to improve the systems that already exist, making them better, faster cheaper. This is sometimes called "Market Pull" Innovation. Radical innovation is more focused on new technologies, new business models and breakthrough businesses. This is sometimes called "Technology Push" Innovation;
- Innovation is people creating value by implementing new ideas;
- The starting point for innovation is the generation of creative ideas. Innovation is the process of taking those ideas to market or to usefulness;
- Innovation is anything that provides a new perceived benefit to a customer or employee;
- Innovation concerns the search for and the discovery, experimentation, development, imitation and adoption of new products, new processes and new organizational set ups;
- Innovation is the conversion of knowledge and ideas into a benefit, which may be for commercial use or for the public good; the benefit may be new or improved products, processes or services;
- Innovation is the process that transforms ideas into commercial value;
- The distinction between "invention" and "innovation" is that invention is the creation of a new idea or concept, and innovation is turning the new concept into commercial success or widespread use;
- Innovation = Invention + Exploitation;

The Origin of Innovation

"Innovation is the result of:

1. A shock (a major failure) to the system,
2. Problemistic search,
3. random variability in experimentation,
4. Deliberate decision to invest in learning,
5. Match between a need and ideas which already exist,
6. Formal vehicles for stimulating innovation such as research and development,
7. Managerial risk seeking or risk averse behaviour,
8. Availability of slack resources,
9. Management philosophy and organizational climate, and
10. Customer needs."

Definition of Innovation

1. "The three stages in the process of innovation: *invention, translation* and *commercialization.*" Bruce D. Merrifield. 1986. ***Forces of Change Affecting High Technology Industries. A speech by U.S. Assistant Secretary of Commerce.***

2. *Invention*: The power of inventing or being invented; ingenuity or creativity; something originating in an experiment. Innovation: the act or process of innovating; something newly introduced, new method, custom, device, etc.;

Change in the way of doing things; renew, alter. ***Webster's New World Dictionary, 1982.***

3. *Phases of Growth*: Entrepreneurial; divergent; inventive; creative; exploratory management; duplication; modification; improvement; commonality/likeness shared leadership; divergence and innovation; sharing and integrating different ness; partnering/vision. "Innovators can hold a situation in chaos for long periods of time without having to reach a resolution...won't give up...have a long-term commitment to their dream...innovators introduce a maximum of tension into the thinking process, unifying concepts that often appear to be opposed, solving problems which appear impossible." ***George Land*** and ***Beth Jarman.***

4. "This (innovation) life cycle is an S-shaped logistic curve consisting of three distinct phases: *emergence* (the development of the product or service, its manufacturing capabilities, and its place in the market), *growth* (where the product family pervades the market), and *maturity* (where the market is saturated and growth slows)." ***William G. Howard, Jr.*** and ***Bruce R. Guile. 1992.***

5. "Innovation cuts across a broad range of activities, institutions and time spans. If any part of the pipeline is broken or constricted, the flow of benefits is slowed. This is felt ultimately in lower productivity and lowered standards of living. In this sense, the cost of capital is crucial not only at the early stages of research and product development but also at the later stages when high-technology products are installed in production processes, in both manufacturing and service industries, as new tools

to improve worker effectiveness." ***James Botkin, Dan Dimancescu*** and ***Ray Stata, 1983.***

6. The four types of Innovations:

   I. Architectural Innovation

   II. Market Innovation

   III. Regular Innovation

   IV. Revolutionary Innovation ***William J. Abernathy, Kim B. Clark,*** and ***Alan M. Kantrow, 1983.***

7. "Continuous innovation occurs largely because a few key executives have a broad vision of what their organizations can accomplish for the world and lead their enterprises toward it. They appreciate the role of innovation in achieving their goals and consciously manage their concerns, value systems and atmospheres to support it." ***James Brian Quinn, 1986.***

8. Five Stages of the Innovation Process:

   1. Recognition

   2. Invention

   3. Development

   4. Implementation

   5. Diffusion ***Modesto A. Maidique, 1980.***

9. "The literature on organizational innovation is rich in lessons...describes processes that are also prevalent in the natural universe. Innovation is fostered by information gathered from new connections; from insights gained by journeys into

other disciplines or places; from active, collegial networks and fluid, open boundaries. Innovation arises from ongoing circles of exchange, where information is not just accumulated or stored, but created. Knowledge is generated anew from connections that weren't there before." ***Margaret J. Wheatley, 1992.***

10. "To explain innovation, we need a new theory of organizational knowledge creation....The cornerstone of our epistemology is the distinction between tacit and explicit knowledge...the key to knowledge creation lies in the mobilization and conversion of tacit knowledge." ***Ikujiro Nonaka*** and ***Hirotaka Takeuchi, 1995.***

Adoption Curves

Ryan and Gross (1943) plotted the number of farmers adopting hybrid corn based on the year farmers adopted it. The data revealed a normal curve. Lionberger (1960) plotted the same type of data on a cumulative basis and revealed an S or growth curve. Both curves indicated a small number of farmers adopted an innovation initially, followed later by the majority of farmers.

Categories of Adopters

Researchers have often assigned titles to individuals based on their adoption behaviour. The best-known scheme is from Rogers (1958). Since the adoption of an agricultural innovation followed a normal curve, he developed classifications of adopters by calculating the mean for the curve and then, by adding or subtracting the standard deviation, divided the curve into five segments. The segments were assigned these categories: Innovators, Early Adopters, Early Majority, Late Majority, and Laggards (Figure 1).

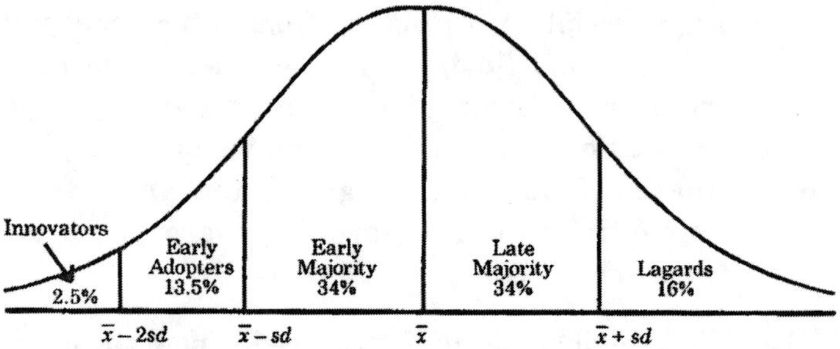

The classic adoption curve indicating a small number of individuals adopting the innovation early (left tail), followed by the majority of adopters. Those adopting last form the right tail of the curve.

Characteristics of Adopters

The literature describes farmers who adopt an innovation early as being different from other farmers. Innovators are younger, more cosmopolitan, have higher incomes than later adopters, and have the largest operations of all adopter categories. In addition, adopter categories differ in their source of information on innovations, with innovators relying on primary sources and later adopters relying on word of mouth.

Characteristics of Innovations

A key part of the adoption process is identifying the criteria used in decision-making. To begin with, the new innovation has to have a relative advantage over the old practice and it has to be consistent with existing cultural patterns.

In addition, researchers identified a number of other characteristics of innovations that relate to their adoption. Innovations that are less complex, are divisible, readily observable, low cost, and profitable are adopted quickly. Innovations that are congruent with previous innovations are also adopted quickly. For instance, hybrid sorghum was adopted at a dramatic rate where hybrid corn was already in general use .

Stages of the Adoption Process

Beal, Rogers, and Bohlen (1957) developed a sequence of stages to describe the adoption process:

- ***Awareness.*** The farmer knows of the existence of the innovation but lacks details.
- ***Information.*** The farmer becomes interested in the innovation and seeks further information.
- ***Evaluation.*** The farmer takes the information about the innovation and weighs the alternatives regarding resources of land, labour, capital, and management ability.
- ***Trial.*** The farmer uses the innovation on a small-scale basis.
- ***Adoption.*** The farmer uses the innovation on a full-scale basis.

Diffusion of Innovation Theory

One of the greatest pains to human nature is the pain of a new idea. It...makes you think that after all, your favourite notions may be wrong, your firmest beliefs ill-founded... Naturally, therefore, common men hate a new idea, and are disposed more or less to ill-treat the original man who brings it.—***Walter Bagehot Physics and Politics.***

Definition of Diffusion of Innovation

In his comprehensive book *Diffusion of Innovation,* Everett Rogers defines diffusion as the process by which an innovation is communicated through certain channels over time among the members of a social system. Rogers' definition contains four elements that are present in the diffusion of innovation process. The ***four main elements are:***

(1) *Innovation.* An idea, practices, or objects that is perceived as knew by an individual or other unit of adoption.

(2) *Communication Channels.* The means by which messages get from one individual to another.

(3) *Time.* The three time factors are:

(a) Innovation-decision process.

(b) Relative time with which an innovation is adopted by an individual or group.

(c) Innovation's rate of adoption.

(4) *Social System.* A set of interrelated units that are engaged in joint problem solving to accomplish a common goal.

Diffusion of Innovation

The original diffusion research was done as early as 1903 by the French Sociologist Gabriel Tarde who plotted the original S-shaped diffusion curve. Tardes' 1903 S-shaped curve is of current importance because "most innovations have an S-shaped rate of adoption" (Rogers, 1983). The variance lies in the slope of the "S". Some new innovations diffuse rapidly creating a steep S-curve; other innovations have a slower rate of adoption, creating a more gradual slope of the S-curve. The rate of adoption, or diffusion rate has become an important area of research to sociologists, and more specifically, to advertisers.

In the 1940's, two sociologists, Bryce Ryan and Neal Gross "published their seminal study of the diffusion of hybrid seed among Iowa farmers" renewing interest in the diffusion of innovation S-curve. The now infamous hybrid-corn study resulted in a renewed wave of research. "The rate of adoption of the agricultural innovation followed an S-shaped normal curve when plotted on a cumulative basis over time". This rate of adoption curve was similar to the S-shaped diffusion curve graphed by Tarde forty years earlier.

The five segments of farmers are:

(1) Innovators,

(2) Early adopters,

(3) Early majority,

(4) Late majority, and

(5) Laggards.

"The first farmers to adopt (the innovators) were more cosmopolite (indicated by travelling more frequently to Des Moines) and of higher socio-economic status than later adopters". One of the most important characteristics of the first segment of a population to adopt an innovation, the innovators, is that they require a shorter adoption period than any other category.

Characteristics dominant in the innovator type:

(1) Venture some, desire for the rash, the daring, and the risky,

(2) Control of substantial financial resources to absorb possible loss from an unprofitable innovation,

(3) The ability to understand and apply complex technical knowledge, and

(4) The ability to cope with a high degree of uncertainty about an innovation.

Characteristics Adopters

(1) Integrated part of the local social system,

(2) Greatest degree of opinion leadership in most systems,

(3) Serve as role model for other members or society,

(4) Respected by peers, and

(5) Successful.

Ideas confine a man to certain social groups and social groups confine a man to certain ideas. Many ideas are more easily changed by aiming at a group than by aiming at an individual.

The Adoption Process

In his book *Diffusion of Innovations*, Rogers defines the diffusion process as one "which is the spread of a new idea from its source of invention or creation to its ultimate users or adopters". Rogers differentiates the adoption process from the diffusion process in that the diffusion process occurs within society, as a group process; whereas, the adoption process is pertains to an individual. Rogers defines "the adoption process as the mental process through which an individual passes from first hearing about an innovation to final adoption".

Five Stages of Adoption

Rogers breaks the adoption process down into five stages. Although, more or fewer stages may exist, Rogers says that "at the present time there seem to be five main functions". The five stages are:

(1) Awareness,

(2) Interest,

(3) Evaluation,

(4) Trial, and

(5) Adoption.

The Innovation-Decision Process

The innovation-decision process as the "process through which an individual (or other decision-making unit such as a group, society, economy, or country) passes through the innovation-decision process".

Five stages in the Innovation-Decision Process:

(1) From first knowledge of innovation,

(2) To forming an attitude toward the innovation,

(3) To a decision to adopt or reject,

(4) To implementation of the new idea,

(5) To confirmation of this decision.

Prior conditions affect the innovation-decision process. such as:

(1) Previous practice,

(2) Felt needs/problems,

(3) Innovativeness, and

(4) Norms of the social systems.

Diffusion research is emerging as a single, integrated body of concepts and generalizations, even though the investigations are conducted by researchers in several scientific discipline.

For the most part, the world of advertising is concerned with the diffusion of innovation process in terms of how such research studies can facilitate product adoption and therefore market segmentation. But it should be mentioned that additional research exists on the diffusion of innovation theory in other scientific disciplines, such as economic development and in the technological sector.

Five Stages of the Diffusion Process

In his book *Inventive Activity, Diffusion, and Stages of Economic Growth,* Stanislav Gomulka identifies five stages of technological growth that any economy in the world can be divided. They are:

(1) By and large balanced growth at a low rate,

(2) Transition phase of gradually increasing the characteristic rate of growth (Gomulka states that there are four characteristic rates of growth),

(3) High level of roughly semi-balanced growth,

(4) Transition phase of gradually decreasing characteristic rate of growth,

(5) By and large balanced growth at a relatively low rate, possibly close to the rate of growth of the country's population.

The diffusion of innovation process consists of four main elements: the innovation, communication through certain channels, over time, and among the members of a social system. Research concerning the diffusion of innovation process has increased significantly the past several decades due to its' versatility. A universality or similarity found amongst the various research studies on the diffusion of innovation process is that the adoption process or the rate of diffusion can be charted on an S-shaped curve.

Of vast importance to those in the advertising field is the innovation-decision process. Rogers defines the innovation-decision process as the process through which an individual passes from first knowledge of an innovation to forming an attitude toward the innovation, to a decision to adopt or reject, to implementation and use of the new idea, and to confirmation of this decision.

The diffusion of innovation process can be tracked on a micro level as is the case of an individual who is a targeted member of an audience, or traced at the macro level when considering economic development or technological advances. In either instance, during the course of the twentieth century the diffusion of innovation theory has proven to be versatile, universal, but most important relevant.

Innovation Decision Process

Different types of learning are involved in extension. Before a group of farmers can decide to try out a new practice, they must first learn of its existence. They may then have to learn some new skills. Five stages can be identified in the process of accepting new ideas.

Awareness. A farmer learns of the existence of the idea but knows little about it.

Interest. The farmer develops interest in the idea and seeks more information about it, from either a friend or the extension agent.

Evaluation. How the idea affects the farmer must now be considered. How will it be of benefit? What are the difficulties or disadvantages of this new idea? The farmer may seek further information or go to a demonstration or meeting, and then decide whether or not to try out the new idea.

Trial. Very often, farmers decide to try the idea on a small scale. For example, they may decide to put manure or fertilizer on a small part of one field and compare the result with the rest of the field. To do this they seek advice on how and when to apply fertilizer or manure.

Adoption. If the farmers are convinced by the trial, they accept the idea fully and it becomes part of their customary way of farming.

Similar stages are involved with individual farmers, farmers' groups, or whole communities. In groups and communities the process is more complex and may take much longer. The extension agent uses a range of extension methods to bring the right kind of information and support to each stage of the process. He must arrange learning experiences that will lead people from one stage to the next. In a community forestry programme, he begins by encouraging people to recognize that there is a problem of declining numbers of trees and that this could be overcome by the community planting and looking after a wood-lot. Interest can then be increased by a visit to another village that has already planted a wood-lot. During the evaluation stage, a lot of discussion will go on in the village. The extension worker can provide detailed information about the costs and returns, and answer questions and doubts. When a decision is taken to do something he can then arrange skill training sessions.

Innovativeness and Adopter Categories

The process by which a new idea spreads among people in an area is known as diffusion. Not all farmers will accept a new idea at the same time. In any rural community, the readiness to accept new ideas and put them into practice varies from farmer to farmer depending on each farmer's previous experience with new ideas, the personality of the farmer and the amount of land and other resources available.

Thus we can identify different categories of farmers in terms of their abilities to adopt new ideas.

Innovators. Innovators are farmers who are eager to accept new ideas. Usually there are only a few people in this class in a farming community. They are often farmers who, having spent some years outside the village, feel that they can make their own decisions without worrying about the opinions of others. In villages, innovators are often looked on with suspicion and jealousy. Yet they are important to the success of an extension programme since they can be persuaded to try new methods and thereby create awareness of them in the community. However, the extension agent should exercise tact and caution, and avoid over praising innovators in public or spending too much time with them. This could result in rejection of the idea by the rest of the community because of jealousy and suspicion of the innovator's motives in adopting new methods.

Early Adopters. Farmers who are more cautious and want to see the idea tried and proved under local conditions are known as early adopters. They express early interest but must first be convinced of the direct benefit of the idea by result demonstration. Usually this group of farmers includes local leaders and others who are respected in the community.

The Majority. If the rest of the farmers adopt a new idea, they will do so more slowly and perhaps less completely. Many farmers will lack the resources to adopt the new idea at all, while others may only do so slowly and with caution. The majority who can and do adopt the idea are likely to be more influenced by the opinions of local leaders and neighbours than by the extension agent or the demonstrations he arranges.

Rate of Adoption

Rate of adoption is the relative speed with which an innovation is adopted by the members of a social system. It is measured by the length of time required for certain per centage of members of a system to adopt an innovative.

The normal rate of progress might require from six to ten years between the introduction of the innovation and its adoption generally through out the community An extension worker who understand this can speed up the operation.

The trick is to get more informal leader to become early adopter and more early adopter to become innovators. This can be done when the people have confidence in the extension worker. The extension worker should develop the confidence of the people in him by providing them satisfying experience.

4

Extension Teaching Methods

Selection of Methods

When choosing a teaching method it is important to know the learners. What are their experiences, interests and goals? When youth are asked what they wish to learn, they may not know enough about a subject to form an opinion. However, if they are involved in selecting goals, they have a stronger sense of ownership. Youth learn best in an atmosphere of warmth and acceptance. They should be actively involved in setting goals and planning their learning activities.

What are the different ways people learn? A visual learner may only need to see an item in writing to remember it. An example is a small child who looks at alphabet cards and can identify the letters. An auditory learner will best be served by having the information spoken to them or repeated by them. By hearing and repeating the 4-H pledge members may quickly learn to associate the words with the four Hs. Kinesthetic learners may need to touch items to determine size, shape, texture, and weight. This allows them to compare and contrast elements as they learn. They can then internalize the concept.

Involving youth in different activities while they learn new material strengthens knowledge retention. This will create new experiences for them to share with others, which also reinforces the learning process. Consider some of the following learning techniques, some of which are traditional.

In the recent past, Extension Training Programme have witnessed vital changes in the training methodology. The old days' training methods like lecture are now being replaced with different multi-dimensional training methods. With the introduction of modern communication techniques, the extension training has received numerous improvements. Senders (1965) commented that to make a training effective it should be based on the fundamentals that people learn by seeing with their own eyes, hearing with their own ears, saying with their mouths and doing with their own hands. Considering the above factors and all the modernization in the field of training methodology, the institute has also incorporated latest training techniques and extension teaching methods. The tentative course content developed by the faculty members is put up before the participants during inaugural session. They are requested to go through the course content and indicate their training need through additions and deletion of any particular topic in course content. After inaugural session, the participants are divided in 2-3 sub-groups to discuss their role and responsibilities while performing the present job and there training needs are assessed.

Selection of Methods

After all extension worker cannot try to choose the best method but can use the combination of methods. These are the following consideration should kept in mind while selecting the best method of teaching.

1. The methods range available to the extension worker.

2. The contribution form method in the programme.
3. Which combination of methods for individual, group and mass media will be best for a specific plan of work.
4. The length of the programme time will be undertaken in the area.
5. Type of programme to be undertaken, i.e., type of information or skills to be imported.
6. The personality and skills of available extension workers.
7. The type of people to be reached, their sex, age, education, motives and other complex characteristics needs to be understood properly.
8. General local conditions, such as seasonal work, weather conditions, available meeting places, organisation and leadership.
9. Financial and other resources, such as equipment, transport and other facilities in using the method.

Programme Delivery Methods

One of the unique features of non-formal education is the large array of methods that can be used for delivering educational programmes. Thus the extension educator has many options that can be used in structuring effective programme delivery systems.

The selection of delivery methods for a programme delivery system should be based on the needs and preferences of the targeted audience and the specific educational purpose. For example, if the objective is to make the general population aware of some innovation, the delivery system might employ several mass media—such as radio, television, newspapers, and magazines—or other methods that can be expected to reach large numbers of people. On the other hand, if the objective is to provide information to targeted clientele who are prepared to test an innovation, the delivery system should emphasize experiential learning methods. Among the experiential methods for which extension clientele have indicated a preference are workshops, Demonstrations, video cassettes, tours, on-farm tests, and field days. Some delivery methods have multiple uses and can be employed effectively at more than one stage in a programme delivery system. Although some methods may be more useful than others, it should be recognized that in most cases it will be necessary to employ more than one method to achieve significant results. Thus when individual methods are selected as components of a programme delivery system, each method should be expected to achieve a purpose in reaching the overall educational objective. For example, a public assembly could open with a symposium in which a few knowledgeable individuals provide information during relatively brief consecutive presentations. Then, if time is available, these individuals could serve as a panel to discuss and clarify the information presented. An alternative is to provide an open discussion period, or forum, at the conclusion of the symposium. This discussion period allows members of the audience to participate and to express their opinions or to ask questions of programme participants or of each other.

Additional supporting information or clarification could be provided by means of fact sheets and other publications, collaborative analysis of data or results, and other delivery methods that provide learner reinforcement. The information presented could also be reinforced or clarified by giving programme participants video-cassettes and audio-cassettes that they can use for home study. These cassettes could provide the learners opportunities to gain greater understanding of the information presented and assist them in applying that information to their own situations. In this example, the methods used are a symposium, forum, panel, fact sheet or other publication, analysis of data results, video-cassettes, and audio-cassettes. As demonstrated, adequate planning combined with creativity in selecting delivery methods provides a systematic design for effectively providing educational opportunities for our targeted audiences. In choosing methods to use in a delivery system, be sure to include enough methods to convey the desired content and accomplish the educational objectives.

A Programme Delivery System

A programme delivery system is a planned and organized structure of individual programme delivery methods that have been chosen for a specific educational purpose and are appropriately integrated to accomplish an educational objective. Extensive learning research has consistently shown that learners need and want to gain some type of experience with new information as well as to be supported and reinforced in the learning process. In the process of receiving information, gaining experience with it, and being reinforced in the learning process, learners need to assimilate or integrate the new information with knowledge they already possess. Thus to promote effective and efficient learning, a delivery system should include methods, whenever possible, that (1) provide desired experiential opportunities for the learner, (2) reinforce the learner, and (3) provide opportunities for the learner to integrate new information with existing knowledge and skills.

In a programme delivery system, the methods considered *experiential* are those that allow the learner to gain experience with or to "feel" the information presented. This experience may occur through physical activity or it may involve the senses, emotions, or social interaction, depending on the content of the educational programme.

Reinforcement delivery methods provide informational, emotional, or social support for the learner to facilitate learning and enhance or maintain the motivation to continue in the learning process.

Table 1. Programme Delivery Methods in Extension Education

Experiential Methods	*Symposium*	*Fax Message*
Audio-cassette	Colloquy	Computer software
Video-cassette	Dialogue	Newsletter
Interactive video	Institute	Letter
Audio compact disk	Buzz group	Home study kit
Video compact disk	Discussion group	
Method demonstration	Brainstorming	Other methods
Result demonstration	Audience reaction team	Broadcast television
On-farm test	Listening team	Cable television
Tour	Interview	Radio
Field day	Teleconference	Newspaper
Workshop	Telephone conversation	Movie (film)
Analysis of data or results	Computer network	Film strip
Game	Satellite conferencing	Slide-tape presentation
Skit	Personal visit	Photograph
Networking	Office visit	Bulletin board
Role play		Show
Case study	Reinforcement methods	Fair
	Fact sheet	Exhibit
Integrative Methods	Notebook	Lecture
Conference	Leaflet or flier	Speech
Convention	Pamphlet or booklet	Teletip message
Seminar	Magazine article	Church bulletin
Panel	Journal article	Comics
Meeting	Poster	Novelty items
	Book	

Programme delivery methods that provide the learner opportunities to discuss, clarify, or otherwise gain greater understanding of new information can be classified as *integrative* methods. These methods generally provide opportunities for learners to merge new information with their existing knowledge.

Table 1 lists delivery methods, divided into four categories: *experiential, reinforcement, integrative,* and other. The three initial categories indicate the stage at which the various delivery methods can be used most effectively in a programme delivery system. The other category lists those methods that are applicable in a wide variety of systems or that can be used for limited or special situations. Obviously, many of the methods listed can fit under more than one category. For example, an audio-cassette can be designed to provide experiential opportunities as well as to reinforce the learner. Therefore, the categories in the table only suggest the best projected use.

To summarize, several factors should be considered when selecting programme delivery methods for a programme delivery system. These factors are:

- The targeted audience
- The educational objective
- The type and content of the message being provided
- The characteristics of the delivery method
- The method's utility for providing desired learning support

Ultimately, you should select those methods that seem most appropriate and logical for meeting the educational needs of the targeted audience, and you should make adjustments as needed based on programme evaluations.

Programme Delivery Methods

Experiential Methods

- *Audio-cassette*—Recorded audio messages that can be listened to at the convenience of the learner.
- *Video-cassette*—A recording on videotape that can provide both visual and audio information.
- *Interactive video*—An electronic system with which the learner can interact to obtain information through both video and audio means.
- *Audio compact disk*—A small, thin disk used for recording and playing back large quantities of audio information.
- *Video compact disk*—A small, thin, disk capable of recording and playing back video and audio information.
- *Method demonstration*—An explanation of how to implement a practice or accomplish a task by showing a practical application or guiding the learner in carrying out the task.
- *Result demonstration*—A presentation that shows the effects of a practice change or task by means of practical application, using visual, experiential, or oral methods; it usually involves a before-and-after comparison.
- *On-farm test*—A process in which an innovative practice or solution to a problem is tested on an actual farm to demonstrate its viability or to test its applicability; the test may employ before-and-after, control-versus-test, or other comparisons.
- *Tour*—Travel by a group of learners to places of defined interest to study innovations, systems,

objects, demonstrations, applied creative programmes, or other items that may be unfamiliar to participants.

- *Field day*—A planned activity of one-day duration in an outdoor setting for demonstrations; observation of programmes, practices, activities, or objects; presentations; or practical experiences.
- *Workshop*—A meeting in which a small group of people with common interests meet to study or research a specific topic or to practice a specific skill to enhance their individual knowledge and proficiency.
- *Analysis of data or results*—Evaluation, use, or presentation of new or existing data to explain or predict the impact of a practice, innovation, input change, or changing conditions and circumstances.
- *Game*—A simulation or fantasy in which learners explore or experience a subject, opportunities, or implications.
- *Skit*—A short, planned, rehearsed, dramatic presentation involving two or more persons designed to present information or illustrate a situation.
- *Networking*—The sharing or exchanging of information through deliberate action on the part of one or more individuals by means of collaborative linkages with other individuals, groups, or organizations.
- *Role play*—An exercise in which selected members of a group are assigned to play specific roles in a hypothetical or simulated situation followed by discussion among all group members.

- *Case study*—A specific and detailed description of an event, situation, or circumstance that is presented to an audience for study and analysis.

Reinforcement Methods

- *Fact sheet*—A publication of six pages or fewer focused on a single subject or a component of a broader topic that presents instructions, guidelines, or other specific information.

- *Notebook*—A compilation of fact sheets or other printed information pertaining to a specific topic.

- *Leaflet or flier*—Brief, concise printed information focused on a specific programme, objective, current event, or other activity and designed to create or enhance awareness.

- *Pamphlet or booklet*—A printed publication that provides more comprehensive information on a subject than a fact sheet, leaflet, or flier.

- *Magazine article*—A means of presenting information to selected audiences via a printed mass medium. Designed to improve understanding of a subject; often accompanied by pictures, graphs, and charts for clarity.

- *Journal article*—A means of presenting scientific, theoretical, or philosophical information in a professional journal.

- *Speciality publication article*—The presentation of information in a periodical that focuses on a specific discipline, commodity, audience, or subject matter.

- *Poster*—A large, printed sheet intended for display and containing words, illustrations, or both to provide general or specific information for broad or targeted audiences.

- *Book*—A comprehensive, bound publication that usually provides thorough treatment of a subject or presentation of a story.

- *Fax message*—Printed information electronically transmitted between two or more points by means of a facsimile machine.

- *Computer software*—A set of instructions, or programme, that enables a computer to be used to provide educational information, to transmit communications, or to aid in decision making.

- *Newsletter*—A printed instrument developed for a targeted audience that is intended to provide timely information of current potential interest to the readers.

- *Letter*—A written message intended for a single individual, usually transmitted in person or by a delivery service such as the U.S. Postal Service or an electronic mail system.

- *Home study kit*—A collection of educational materials created or assembled for independent study on a specific subject.

Integrative Methods

- *Conference*—A meeting of a large or small group of people having similar interests for formal presentations to the entire group and for smaller group sessions that focus on specific components of the general topic.

- *Convention*—An assembly of a large number of people who have similar interests and who represent subsets of a larger organization. Multiple planned meetings of subgroups occur simultaneously at least part of the time during the event.

- *Seminar*—A meeting in which a group of people who are studying a specific subject engage in discussions led by a recognized authority.

- *Panel*—A discussion among a small group of people who are knowledgeable about a subject conducted in front of an audience. Panel members make no formal presentation; they exchange ideas through conversation.

- *Forum*—A form of group discussion that allows audience members to participate. The discussion period may be completely open or restricted to a specific part of the programme.

- *Meeting*—An assembly of people at which information on a topic of common interest is presented.

- *Symposium*—An assembly in which short presentations are made by a small number of speakers who are knowledgeable about a particular subject. These presentations may range from 5 to 20 minutes each.

- *Colloquy*—A gathering at which a panel of individuals discuss a subject in front of an audience but interact with audience members only when those members wish to ask a specific question or clarify a point under discussion. When a particular point is resolved, the organized discussion among panel members continues.

- *Dialogue*—A discussion between two people conducted in front of an audience.

- *Institute*—A planned series of sessions of one or more days each for in-depth presentations and significant study by individuals who hold similar interests.

- *Buzz group*—A group of five to eight persons who discuss relevant questions posed by the leader of a larger group assembly.
- *Discussion group*—An informal meeting of people to discuss a topic of mutual concern.
- *Brainstorming*—A process in which members of an audience are encouraged to participate by sharing their ideas or suggestions on a subject. No discussion of each point is allowed until all ideas have been expressed.
- *Audience reaction team*—Three members of the audience pre-selected to respond to the information presented by offering a brief summary and interpretation. The team provides an opportunity for group reaction or response when the audience is large or time is limited.
- *Listening team*—A small group formed from members of an audience before a presentation and asked to listen for different things in the presentation and then to discuss or clarify how the information could be applied.
- *Interview*—A face-to-face meeting in which facts and beliefs are elicited or exchanged.
- *Teleconferencing*—The process by which three or more individuals at distant locations are connected by two-way audio signals or audio and video signals for the purpose of exchanging information and ideas.
- *Telephone conversation*—An electronic means for direct sharing of information between two people at distant locations by voice transmission.
- *Computer network*—The linking of three or more computers for the purpose of sharing and

exchanging information. The linkage may be restricted to the computers on the local network or may extend to other information sources over a wide area.

- *Satellite conferencing*—A teleconferencing method that uses both audio and video signals transmitted via cable or satellite for the purpose of conferring, instructing, and disseminating information among people at distant locations.
- *Personal visit*—A face-to-face exchange of information between two or more people, usually at the location of the person or persons receiving the information.
- *Office visit*—A face-to-face exchange of information among two or more people, usually at the location of the information provider.

Other Methods

- *Broadcast television*—A means of providing audio and visual messages to mass audiences within a broad reception area by means of a central transmitting station and individual receivers at the location of each audience member.
- *Cable television*—A system in which television signals are distributed through an electronic cable to those who subscribe to the service, usually restricted to a relatively small geographic area. This feature makes it possible to transmit information selectively to a defined audience.
- *Radio*—A means of providing information to mass audiences via sound messages communicated through a central transmitting station and individual receivers at the location of each audience member.

- *Newspaper*—A printed periodical publication, usually issued daily or weekly, that provides information directed to a broad audience within a specific geographical region.
- *Movie (film)*—The recording of audio and visual images on film in a way that allows information to be presented in real-life-paced motion.
- *Film strip*—A system for presenting a series of images structured in a specific order on 35-millimeter film to be projected for viewing by a group.
- *Slide-tape presentation*—A system in which 35-millimeter slides are projected in synchronization with an audio tape to provide simultaneous audio and visual information.
- *Photograph*—A print image used to provide visual information.
- *Bulletin board*—A physical medium to which messages can be attached to provide information to anyone who notices.
- *Show*—An event in which experiences or information is transferred to specific audiences or to the general public via exhibits, competitions, demonstrations, or other items or activities.
- *Fair*—A planned event for a large audience for the purpose of exhibiting, observing, buying, selling, entertaining, educating, or informing.
- *Exhibit*—A display of materials or objects designed to inform.
- *Lecture*—An oral presentation, usually formal in nature, to a group by an individual highly knowledgeable about the subject.

- *Speech*—A formal presentation of information or opinions by an individual to a group; it does not necessarily involve any further interaction between the speaker and the audience.
- *Tele tip message*—An informative audio message on a single topic accessed by individuals through the telephone by dialing a toll-free number.
- *Church bulletin*—A means for providing brief printed information to limited audiences.
- *Puppet*—A means of presenting information via the performance of inanimate fictional characters.
- *Comics*—The use of cartoons to attract attention, create interest, or provide information. This method is especially useful for special or handicapped audiences.
- *Novelty items*—Presentation of a brief message printed on objects such as key chains, pencils, canes, caps, cups, or other similar items.

Information about Instructional Methods

Instructional methods and teaching methods mean the same thing; although some may argue otherwise, to split hairs over these terms adds nothing to the process of learning to be a teacher. Direct and indirect instruction are two main categories that many educators find useful for classifying teaching methods, but it is, as you will see, a bit more complicated than placing all instruction into two categories. Any instructional method a teacher uses has advantages, disadvantages, and requires some preliminary preparation. Often times, a particular teaching method will naturally flow into another, all within the same lesson, and excellent teachers have developed the skills to make the process seamless to the students. Which instructional method is "right" for a particular lesson depends on many things, and among them are the age and developmental level of the students, what the students already know, and what they need to know to succeed with the lesson, the subject-matter content, the objective of the lesson, the available people, time, space and material resources, and the physical setting. Another, more difficult problem is to select an instructional method that best fits one's particular teaching style and the lesson-situation. There is no one "right" method for teaching a particular lesson, but there are some criteria that pertain to each that can help a teacher make the best decision possible. The following teaching or instructional methods relate to the instruction. The methods are not listed in a preferred sequence, no hierarchy of putative superiority of method is intended, and obviously, not all are appropriate for all grades and subject matter content DIRECT TEACHING.

Advantages	*Disadvantages*	*Preparation*
Very specific learning targets. Students are told reasons why content is important-helps to clarify lesson objective. Relatively easy to measure student gains. Is a widely accepted instructional method. Good for teaching specific facts and basic skills.	Can stifle teacher creativity. Requires well-organized content preparation and good oral communication skills. Steps must be followed in prescribed order. May not be effective for higher-order thinking skills, depending on the knowledge base and skill of the teacher.	Content must be organized in advance. Teacher should have infor-information about student prerequisites for the lesson.

Lecture-cum-Discussion

The participants of the training courses conducted by this Institute usually are Master Trainers/Scientists of State Agricultural Universities and State, Distt. and Sub-Divisional level Extension Officers from State Govts. Since the adult/ senior people do not relish too much listening to others, the talk-cum-discussion method is used to orient the participants about concept of a particular module during the training session. The opportunity is provided to the participants to discuss their field experiences and problems related to the particular module. This method is used for the modules on extension talk, skill teaching, Audio-visual aids and other topics like communication process and broad based agricultural extension etc.

Discussion

A way to create an exchange of ideas is to provide two way communication through discussion. The educator speaks directly to a learner, asks questions or makes comments, then waits for a response. This helps auditory learners retain the material.

Another setting may allow a group of learners to either take a stand on an issue or be assigned a position. The groups can then discuss their views with each other. Continuing this open conversation enables learners to express themselves and may provide new areas for learning.

Small Group Discussion

Strengths

- Allows participation of everyone
- People often more comfortable in small groups
- Can reach group consensus

Limitations

- Needs careful thought as to purpose of group
- Groups may get side tracked

Preparation

- Needs to prepare specific tasks or questions for group to answer

Lecture

Strengths

- Presents factual material in direct, logical manner
- Contains experience which inspires
- Stimulates thinking to open discussion
- Useful for large groups

Limitations

- Experts are not always good teachers
- Audience is passive
- Learning is difficult to gauge
- Communication in one way

Preparation

- Needs clear introduction and summary
- Needs time and content limit to be effective
- Should include examples, anecdotes

Lecture with Discussion

Strengths

- Involves audience at least after the lecture
- Audience can question, clarify and challenge

Limitations

- Time may limit discussion period
- Quality is limited to quality of questions and discussion

Preparation

- Requires that questions be prepared prior to discussion

Panel of Experts

Strengths

- Allows experts to present different opinions
- Can provoke better discussion than a one person discussion
- Frequent change of speaker keeps attention from lagging

Limitations

- Experts may not be good speakers
- Personalities may overshadow content
- Subject may not be in logical order

Preparation

- Facilitator coordinates focus of panel, introduces and summarizes
- Briefs panel

Brainstorming

Strengths

- Listening exercise that allows creative thinking for new ideas
- Encourages full participation because all ideas equally recorded
- Draws on group's knowledge and experience

- Spirit of congeniality is created
- One idea can spark off other other ideas

Limitations

- Can be unfocused
- Needs to be limited to 5-7 minutes
- People may have difficulty getting away from known reality
- If not facilitated well, criticism and evaluation may occur

Preparation

- Facilitator selects issue
- Must have some ideas if group needs to be stimulated

Videotapes

Strengths

- Entertaining way of teaching content and raising issues
- Keep group's attention
- Looks professional
- Stimulates discussion

Limitations

- Can raise too many issues to have a focused discussion
- Discussion may not have full participation
- Only as effective as following discussion

Preparation

- Need to set up equipment
- Effective only if facilitator prepares questions to discuss after the show

Class Discussion

Strengths

- Pools ideas and experiences from group
- Effective after a presentation, film or experience that needs to be analyzed
- Allows everyone to participate in an active process

Limitations

- Not practical with more that 20 people
- Few people can dominate
- Others may not participate
- Is time consuming
- Can get off the track

Preparation

- Requires careful planning by facilitator to guide discussion
- Requires question outline

Small Group Discussion

Strengths

- Allows participation of everyone
- People often more comfortable in small groups
- Can reach group consensus

Limitations

- Needs careful thought as to purpose of group
- Groups may get side tracked

Preparation

- Needs to prepare specific tasks or questions for group to answer

Case Studies

Strengths

- Develops analytic and problem solving skills
- Allows for exploration of solutions for complex issues
- Allows student to apply new knowledge and skills

Limitations

- People may not see relevance to own situation
- Insufficient information can lead to inappropriate results

Preparation

- Case must be clearly defined in some cases
- Case study must be prepared

Role Playing

Placing learners into roles where they act out ideas and reactions can be rewarding. By active involvement, learners of different types will retain more than if they merely sat and watched a skit or video performance. Each group differs in how the message is delivered and interpreted. If the educator is trying to make certain points in the exercise which are not obvious, then additional processing and discussion of the material may be required.

Strengths

- Introduces problem situation dramatically
- Provides opportunity for people to assume roles of others and thus appreciate another point of view
- Allows for exploration of solutions
- Provides opportunity to practice skills

Limitations

- People may be too self-conscious
- Not appropriate for large groups
- People may feel threatened

Preparation

- Trainer has to define problem situation and roles clearly
- Trainer must give very clear instructions

Report-Back Sessions

Strengths

- Allows for large group discussion of role plays, case studies, and small group exercise
- Gives people a chance to reflect on experience
- Each group takes responsibility for its operation

Limitations

- Can be repetitive if each small group says the same thing

Preparation

- Trainer has to prepare questions for groups to discuss

Worksheets/Surveys

Strengths

- Allows people to thing for themselves without being influences by others
- Individual thoughts can then be shared in large group

Limitations

- Can be used only for short period of time

Preparation

- Facilitator has to prepare handouts

Index Card Exercise

Strengths

- Opportunity to explore difficult and complex issues

Limitations

- People may not do exercise

Preparation

- Facilitator must prepare questions

Guest Speaker

Strengths

- Personalizes topic
- Breaks down audience's stereotypes

Limitations

- May not be a good speaker

Preparation

- Contact speakers and coordinate
- Introduce speaker appropriately

Values Clarification Exercise

Strengths

- Opportunity to explore values and beliefs
- Allows people to discuss values in a safe environment
- Gives structure to discussion

Limitation

- People may not be honest
- People may be too self-conscious

Preparation

- Facilitator must carefully prepare exercise
- Must give clear instructions
- Facilitator must prepare discussion questions

Cooperative Learning

Advantages	*Disadvantages*	*Preparation*
Helps foster mutual responsibility. Supported by research as an effective technique. Students learn to be patient, less critical and more compassionate.	Some students don't work well this way. Loners find it hard to share answers. Aggressive students try to take over. Bright students tend to act superior.	Decide what skills or knowledge are to be learned. Requires some time to prepare students to learn how to work in groups.

Lecture

Advantages	*Disadvantages*	*Preparation*
Factual material is presented in a direct, logical manner. May provide experiences that inspire —useful for large groups.	Proficient oral skills are necessary. Audience is often passive. Learning is difficult to gauge. Communication is one-way. Not appropriate for children below grade 4.	There should be a clear introduction and summary. Effectiveness related to time and scope of content. Is always audience specific; often includes examples, anecdotes.

Lecture with Discussion

Advantages	*Disadvantages*	*Preparation*
Involves students, at least after the lecture. Students can question, clarify and challenge. Lecture can be interspersed with discussion.	Time constraints may affect discussion opportunities. Effectiveness is connected to appropriate questions and discussion; often requires teacher to "shift gears" quickly.	Teacher should be prepared to allow questions during lecture, as appropriate. Teacher should also anticipate difficult questions and prepare appropriate responses in advance.

Panel of Experts

Advantages	*Disadvantages*	*Preparation*
Experts present different opinions. Can provoke better discussion than a one person discussion. Frequent change of speaker keeps attention from lagging.	Personalities may overshadow content. Experts are often not effective speakers. Subject may not be in logical order. Not appropriate for elementary age students. Logistics can be troublesome.	Teacher coordinates focus of panel, introduces and summarizes. Teacher briefs panel.

Brainstorming

Advantages	*Disadvantages*	*Preparation*
Listening exercise that allows creative thinking for new ideas.	Can be unfocused. Needs to be limited to 5-7 minutes.	Teacher selects issue. Teacher must be ready to intervene when the

(Contd.)

(Contd. Table)

Advantages	*Disadvantages*	*Preparation*
Encourages full participation because all ideas are equally recorded. Draws on group's knowledge and experience. Spirit of cooperation is created. One idea can spark off other ideas.	Students may have difficulty getting away from known reality. If not managed well, criticism and negative evaluation may occur. Value to students depends in part on their maturity level.	process is hopelessly bogged doen.

Videotapes/Slides

Advantages	*Disadvantages*	*Preparation*
Entertaining way of introducing content and raising issues. Usually keeps group's attention. Looks professional Stimulates discussion.	Can raise too many issues to have a focused discussion. Discussion may not have full participation. Most effective when following discussion.	Need to obtain and set up equipment. Effective only if teacher prepares for discussion after the presentation.

Discussion

Advantages	*Disadvantages*	*Preparation*
Pools ideas and experiences from group. Effective after a presentation, film or experience that needs to be analyzed. Allows everyone to participate in an active process.	Not practical with more that 20 students. A few students can dominate. Some students may not participate. Is time consuming can get off the track.	Requires careful planning by teacher to guide discussion. Requires question outline.

Small Group Discussion

Advantages	*Disadvantages*	*Preparation*
Allows for participation of everyone. Students often more comfortable in small groups. Groups can reach consensus.	Needs careful thought as to purpose of group. Groups may get side tracked	Need to prepare specific tasks or questions for group to answer.

Case Studies

Advantages	*Disadvantages*	*Preparation*
Develops analytic and problem solving skills. Allows for exploration of solutions for complex issues. Allows student to apply new knowledge and skills.	Students may not see relevance to own situation. Insufficient information can lead to inappropriate results. Not appropriate for elementary level.	Case must be clearly defined. Case study must be prepared.

Role Playing

Advantages	*Disadvantages*	*Preparation*
Introduces problem situation dramatically. Provides opportunity for students to assume roles of others and thus appreciate another point of view. Allows for exploration of solutions. Provides opportunity to practice skills.	Some students may be too self-conscious. Not appropriate for large groups. Some students may feel threatened.	Teacher has to define problem situation and roles clearly. Teacher must give very clear instructions.

Worksheet/Surveys

Advantages	*Disadvantages*	*Preparation*
Allows students to think for themselves without being influenced by others. Individual thoughts can then be shared in large group.	Can be used only for short period of time.	Teacher has to prepare handouts.

Guest Speakers

Advantages	*Disadvantages*	*Preparation*
Personalizes topic. Breaks down audience's stereotypes.	May not be a good speaker.	Contact speakers and coordinate. Introduce speaker appropriately.

Values Clarification

Advantages	*Disadvantages*	*Preparation*
Opportunity to explore values and beliefs. Allows students to discuss values in a safe environment. Gives structure to discussion.	Students may not be honest about their values. Students may be too self-conscious. Students may not be able to articulate their values in an effective way.	Teacher must carefully prepare exercise. Teacher must give clear instructions Teacher must prepare discussion questions.

Teaching with Slides

I have observed over the years that while slides can add to a class, they bring their own challenges. For example, some students go to sleep after a few slides. I have seen students getting excited about slides and want to engage in a conversation with their instructor and peers, only to be shushed so that more slides can be shown. Slides are not an end in themselves. When students are required merely to remember and reproduce the lecture material accompanying slides, it encourages low-level cognitive skills. Higher-level cognitive activity encourages students to analyze the ideas of others and generate their own. When memorizing slides and lecture material is the main focus of the class, rather than using them as a stimulus for analysis and discussion of main course ideas, they can detract from student learning.

Pre-viewing

- Rehearse the points you want to make about each slide; include questions to direct student attention, and activities to encourage student participation.

Viewing

- Direct student attention. Give them a question to answer as they view the slides (e.g., in the next few slides, how is beauty [or women, etc.] portrayed?)
- Do not turn the classroom lights all the way off.

- Do not use more than five slides in a row, or view multiple slides for more than five minutes at a time.

Post-viewing

- Leave an empty slot after every few slides. The projector will shut off automatically when a blank slot is left between slides, allowing for discussion. At that point, stop and have students discuss or write a brief analysis of what they have been viewing. For example, tell them to discuss with their neighbour or take two minutes to write, "How does the idea of beauty in these slides compare with current conceptions of beauty?"

Less is more. Students learn more when they view fewer slides, but have more time to analyze and interpret them. Discussions, short writing assignments, and application exercises will reinforce concepts and increase learning from slides.

We can help you design activities to get your students actively thinking about your slides—and it only takes a few minutes.

Technology for Teaching

The technology for presenting instructional materials and enhancing communication has been rapidly changing in recent years, but it is important to remain focused on the pedagogic rather than the "gee-whiz" value of technology in your class. Technology can make presentations more effective by introducing information in various new and interesting ways. The key to successful use of technology in instruction is to know the learning objective before choosing a technical tool. Technology can help your students to learn better if you plan it carefully to support specific learning objectives.

Presentation Technology

All classrooms should have an overhead projector. If you plan to use any other presentation technology in your teaching, whether it be videotapes, 35 mm slides, 16mm films, computer display, etc., communicate the special attributes needed in the room you may be assigned to teach in to your departmental scheduling officer. These attributes may include such things as room darkening capabilities, ability to project dual slide images, active network connections, etc.

Video and Film

Most of our students have a great deal of experience passively watching video for entertainment. If you want them to actively watch video for educational purposes, you must help them to change their viewing habits. There are three stages to using video, film and other media in class:

Prior to Viewing

- Introduce the video/film by providing an overview of its content, a rationale of how it relates to the current topic being studied, and a reason students need to know about it.

- Direct student attention to specific aspects of the presentation, possibly by asking them questions beforehand that will be discussed following the presentation.

Viewing

- Show only the relevant sections of a video/film, rather than the entire piece, for best use of class time and greatest impact.

- It may also be appropriate to stop the video/film at appropriate points for discussion or clarification.

Post-Viewing

- Follow up a video/film with an activity that allows students to respond to or extend ideas presented.

- Discussions, short writing assignments, or application exercises, for example, will reinforce the concepts and increase learning from classroom media.

Several collections of films/videos are available for use in your classes. The Classroom Technology Services division of Instructional Support Services has a collection of curriculum oriented videos and 16mm films

Media equipment for classroom use, as well as training and support for faculty who teach in classrooms with installed technology, is available from Classroom Technology Services. Mobile equipment available includes TVs and VCRs, large screen video projectors, computer LCD display panels, laptop computers and peripherals (for classroom use only), laserdisc players, stereo CD and audiocassette players, 16mm projectors and operators, slide and overhead projectors, and record players. 855-8765, option 3.

Designating Roles in Groups

Groups that are created for in-class discussion can be easily organized around the following four-person model. Each member of the group plays a specific role that supports the team's collaborative effort. These roles include:

- ***Leader.*** Responsible keeping the group on task, maintaining the schedule (meetings, deadlines), and maintaining contact information (phone numbers, emails).

- ***Encourager.*** Encourages conversation and inclusion of all opinions, and guides the discussion towards consensus.

- ***Prober.*** Ensures that the assumptions are correct and that there is sufficient evidence for the solution.

- ***Recorder.*** Writes down the group's solution that will be submitted for the group grade.

While some people will tend to lead and some will tend to follow, everyone should be willing to compromise and modify their ideas in the interest of group unity.

If the groups are going to be working together on a long-term project or multiple tasks, you may wish to modify these roles to emulate roles that one might encounter in your discipline. Ensure that the students rotate through these positions. Try to break a long project into at least as many tasks as there are people in each group and have the students rotate through the roles each time they start a new task.

Reporting Group Results

Students should share the results of their group with the class at large. They can do so verbally, on newsprint flipchart, blackboard or overhead, through photocopies, or web pages. Even if they are reporting in printed or electronic format, be sure to have some presentations in class. You do not have to hear from everyone; calling on a few groups at random makes everyone prepare in case they are picked to discuss their project. Use this time to give feedback and debrief the students as to the lessons they might have learned from the group work.

Teaching with the Case Method

Cases are narratives, situations, select data samplings, or statements that present unresolved and provocative issues, situations, or questions. As a teaching/learning tool, cases challenge participants to analyze, critique, make judgments, speculate and express reasoned opinions. Above all, although information can be real or invented, a case must be realistic and believable. The information included must be rich enough to make the situation credible, but not so complete as to close off discussion or exploration. Cases can be short for brief classroom discussions, or long and elaborate for semester-long projects. Cases are important for bringing real world problems into a classroom or a workshop—they ensure active participation and may lead to innovative solutions to problems.

Formats for Cases

- "Finished" cases based on facts—for analysis only, since the solution is indicated or alternate solutions are suggested.

- "Unfinished" open-ended cases, where the results are not yet clear (either because the case has not come to a factual conclusion in real life, or because the instructor has eliminated the final facts.) Students must predict, make choices and offer suggestions that will affect the outcome.

- Fictional cases entirely written by the instructor—can be open-ended or finished. Cautionary note: the case must be both complex enough to mimic reality, yet not have so many "red herrings" as to obscure the goal of the exercise.

- Original documents—news articles, reports with data and statistics, summaries, excerpts from historical writings, artifacts, literary passages, video and audio recordings, ethnographies, etc. With the right questions, these can become problem-solving opportunities. Comparison between two original documents related to the same topic or theme is a strong strategy for encouraging both analysis and synthesis. This gives the opportunity for presenting more than one side of an argument, making the conflicts more complex.

Managing a Case Assignment

- Design discussions for small groups: 3-6 students is an ideal group size for setting up a discussion on a case.

- Design the narrative or situation such that it requires participants to reach a judgment, decision, recommendation, prediction or other concrete outcome. If possible, require each group to reach a consensus on the decision requested.

- Structure the discussion. The instructor should provide a series of written questions to guide small group discussion. Pay careful attention to the sequencing of the questions. Early questions might ask participants to make observations about the facts of the case. Later questions could ask for comparisons, contrasts, and analyses of competing observations or hypotheses. Final questions might ask students to take a position on the matter. The purpose of these questions is to stimulate, guide or prod (but not dictate) participants' observations and analyses. The questions should be impossible to answer with a simple yes or no.

- Debrief the discussion to compare group responses. Help the whole class interpret and understand the implications of their solutions.

Allow groups to work without instructor interference. The instructor must be comfortable with ambiguity and with adopting the non-traditional roles of witness and resource, rather than authority.

Designing Case Study Questions

Cases can be more or less "directed" by the kinds of questions asked—these kinds of questions can be appended to any case, or could be a handout for participants unfamiliar with case studies on how to approach one.

- What is the situation—what do you actually know about it from reading the case? (Distinguishes between fact and assumptions÷critical understanding)

- What issues are at stake? (Opportunity for linking to theoretical readings)

- What questions do you have—what information do you still need? Where/how could you find it?
- What problem(s) need to be solved? (Opportunity to discuss communication versus conflict, gaps between assumptions, sides of the argument)
- What are all the possible options? What are the pros/cons of each option?
- What are the underlying assumptions for [person X] in the case—where do you see them?
- What criteria should you use when choosing an option? What does that mean about your assumptions?

Managing Discussion and Debate Effectively

- Delay the problem-solving part until the rest of the discussion has had time to develop. Start with expository questions to clarify the facts, then move to analysis, and finally to evaluation, judgment, and recommendations.
- Shift points of view: "Now that we've seen it from [W's] standpoint, what's happening here from [Y's] standpoint?" What evidence would support Y's position? What are the dynamics between the two positions?
- Shift levels of abstraction: if the answer to the question above is "It's just a bad situation for her," quotations help: When [Y] says "_____," what are her assumptions? Or seek more concrete explanations: Why does she hold this point of view?"

Group Work

- Ask for benefits/disadvantages of a position; for all sides.

- *Shift time frame*—not just to "What's next?" but also to "How could this situation have been different?" What could have been done earlier to head off this conflict and turn it into a productive conversation? Is it too late to fix this? What are possible leverage points for a more productive discussion? What good can come of the existing situation?

- *Shift to another context:* We see how a person who thinks X would see the situation. How would a person who thinks Y see it? We see what happened in the Johannesburg news, how could this be handled in [your town/province]? How might [insert person, organization] address this problem?

- *Follow-up questions:* "What do you mean by ___?" Or, "Could you clarify what you said about ___?" (even if it was a pretty clear statement—this gives students time for thinking, developing different views, and exploration in more depth). Or "How would you square that observation with what [name of person] pointed out?"

- Point out and acknowledge differences in discussion—"that's an interesting difference from what Sam just said, Sarah. Let's look at where the differences lie" (let sides clarify their points before moving on).

Having the students work in a group encourages discussion among the students. Speaking in front of the whole class can be scary and combined with the tension of speaking to the teacher, the situation can be downright terrifying to students. Breaking them up into groups not only builds develops social skills useful in the professional environment for which they are training, but according to Astin (1993), it is also is one of the three most important ways to make a positive difference in learning at the college level.

Organizing the Groups

Keep in mind the following elements of group work when selecting the appropriate type of group work for your class.

- ***Size:*** Two to six people in a group is ideal. The smaller the group, the more likely each student will be to contribute to the discussion. Groups of two or three students are sufficient for simple tasks where consensus will be reached quickly. Groups of four to six are better for more complex tasks in which the greater number of ideas may improve the final results.

- ***Selection:*** You should either assign students randomly to groups (which limits cliques) or select students so that each group has an equal distribution of talents.

- ***Duration:*** Use the groups for a brief discussion in class or for all semester. Long-term groups work more substantively and less superficially.

To prevent problems with group interaction, you should spend a few minutes discussing the students' roles and expectations for the work .

Designating Roles in Groups

Groups that are created for in-class discussion can be easily organized around the following four-person model. Each member of the group plays a specific role that supports the team's collaborative effort. These roles include:

- ***Leader:*** Responsible keeping the group on task, maintaining the schedule (meetings, deadlines), and maintaining contact information (phone numbers, emails).

- ***Encourager:*** Encourages conversation and inclusion of all opinions, and guides the discussion towards consensus.

- ***Prober:*** Ensures that the assumptions are correct and that there is sufficient evidence for the solution.
- ***Recorder:*** Writes down the group's solution that will be submitted for the group grade.

While some people will tend to lead and some will tend to follow, everyone should be willing to compromise and modify their ideas in the interest of group unity.

If the groups are going to be working together on a long-term project or multiple tasks, you may wish to modify these roles to emulate roles that one might encounter in your discipline. Ensure that the students rotate through these positions. Try to break a long project into at least as many tasks as there are people in each group and have the students rotate through the roles each time they start a new task.

Reporting Group Results

Students should share the results of their group with the class at large. They can do so verbally, on newsprint flipchart, blackboard or overhead, through photocopies, or web pages. Even if they are reporting in printed or electronic format, be sure to have some presentations in class. You do not have to hear from everyone; calling on a few groups at random makes everyone prepare in case they are picked to discuss their project. Use this time to give feedback and debrief the students as to the lessons they might have learned from the group work.

Lecturing

Lecturing is often equated with college teaching. This is rapidly changing, however, as university instructors have begun to recognize that not all students benefit from lecture, nor is lecture the most efficient way to disseminate information. Originally the "lecturer" read to an audience because access to written material was limited, and many of the learners were illiterate. The printing process, digitalized information, and general literacy have dramatically changed the lecturer's function.

Lecturing still has its rightful place among dozens of other teaching techniques, but the question one has to ask is, "Which technique will do most to help students learn?" Some topics lend themselves much more naturally to lecturing than others. The lecture is valid for these reasons: to provide structure and organization to scattered material; to help pace student learning; to reinforce assigned reading by providing an alternative perspective or source of Preparing Lectures.

Being in the same room with someone saying something is not equivalent to learning it. Students must engage the material to retain it. Also, given that students' attention span is around 15 to 20 minutes long and university classes last 50 to 75 minutes, you need to do something to control their attention. Lectures should be punctuated with periodic activities. Many IU instructors report that when they intersperse short lectures with active engagement for students for as brief a time as two to five minutes, students seem to become re-energized for the next 15 to 20 minute mini-lecture.

Planning a Lecture

When you start to plan a lecture, first consider your audience. Undergraduate students represent a broad cross-section of backgrounds and skills, and as a result may arrive at college with varying levels of competence. You neither want to talk over their heads nor to patronize them. You will be more effective if you try as much as possible to draw on knowledge they already have or appeal to experiences that, by analogy, suit the topic.

Before preparing the lecture, ask yourself: how does the lecture fit into the course as a whole? What are your objectives? Do you want to provide the students with an overview of the subject, give them some background information, or provoke them into further contemplation?

Once you've decided that the nature of your topic is indeed suitable for a lecture and have considered both your objectives and the knowledge level of your audience, you still want to make sure that what you need to cover will fit within the time allotted. A typical instructor lament is that there is so much material and so little time. Good organization will enable you to eliminate irrelevant material so that you may cover important points more thoroughly. One award-winning IU faculty member told us that "I believe in the 'few things' approach. Rather than going through a lot of topics, I cover a few in great depth. Having students stay with a few topics÷ provides a longer-lasting learning experience than jumping through a lot of different things" (Middendorf et. al., 1990).

Another IU professor tells us that in 20 years of teaching a large introductory lecture course, he has gradually eliminated 75 per cent of the material he tried to cover. He thinks it is much better for his students to really learn a little than for them to be buried under too much.

Analyzing the Audience

A lecture should be designed with the student's perspective in mind. What are students' current knowledge, assumptions, biases, and, perhaps, misconceptions about the topic? In planning the lecture, you will need to find a way to build on the knowledge students bring, and also provide a means for students to reflect upon their biases and misconceptions. The lecture overall should be planned to answer the question, "How will students' understanding be different at the end of the presentation?"

Generating an Outline

Once you have determined your subject and what your students' needs are, formulate one general question that covers the heart of it, one you could answer in a single lecture. Take time to write it down and study it. Then generate three or four points that you could develop to answer this question. Note these down under the question. You are now gazing at your lecture outline.

Choosing Examples

Your next task is to define the elements of your key points and generate effective examples or analogies for each. Examples generated "on the spur of the moment" in class tend to be trivial; if prepared in advance, examples can both illustrate a particular point and broaden students' understanding of the subject. Think the examples through carefully and consider ways to illustrate them with chalkboard diagrams, slides, overhead transparencies, demonstrations, or case studies, any of which can increase students' understanding and interest.

Choosing Learning Activities

To effectively teach concepts, we must tell our students the generality or rule and give them specific and carefully considered examples. However, that is not enough. If they are to learn the concept in a usable way, we must provide them with a chance to practice using it. For example, in an anthropology lecture on "ethnocentrism," students could be asked to list foods from other countries that they find disgusting. Then, you could give them a list of things Americans eat that are unacceptable to people from other cultures (biscuits and gravy!). The value of this type of exercise is that it helps students to make connections between ideas and to create structures of meaning out of what otherwise might be merely a large number of unrelated facts.

Reviewing the Material

Demonstrating that you know more than your students is easy; teaching is more difficult. Keep in mind that how you relate the material to students will determine your effect as a teacher more than will your ability to generate perfect, complete answers to every question students ask.

However, you will need to develop comfort with the material you are teaching, even if you are confronting it yourself for the first time. Ideally, you will be assigned to a course in the area of your particular expertise, but you should still review material to refresh your memory, and you might try explaining it to someone else as a way of anticipating students' questions and problems.

Delivering the Lecture

Your lecture will be more effective if you remember a number of points about the style and clarity of presentation.

The following suggestions can help ensure that your lecture is clear and well received .

- ***Speak Clearly and Loudly Enough to be Heard.*** This may seem obvious but undoubtedly we have all sinned against this prescription. Talk as though you are talking to the person sitting in the very back of the room. Perhaps in the very first class you should suggest that people signal you if they cannot hear, e.g., cup a hand behind an ear.

- ***Speak Slowly.*** Most of us tend to speak more rapidly when nervous, and this makes many lectures difficult to follow. We also do not notice how fast we are speaking unless it is pointed out or we hear ourselves on tape. Slow down.

- ***Avoid distracting Mannerisms.*** Verbal tics like "ah" or " you know," straightening your notes or tie, etc. Use a videotape early in the semester to help you identify mannerisms that you want to shed.

- ***Provide an Introduction.*** Begin with a concise statement, something that will preview the lecture. Give the listeners a set or frame of reference for the remainder of your presentation. Refer to previous lectures. Attract and focus their attention. Try a broad question to students or a survey of opinions to help draw student attention to your presentation.

- ***Present an Outline.*** Write it on the chalkboard, or use an overhead transparency, or a handout. Then be sure that you refer to it as you move from point to point in your lecture.

- ***Emphasize Principles and Generalizations.*** Research suggests that these are what people really remember—and what you probably really want to teach.

- ***Repeat Your Points in Two or Three Different Ways.*** Your listeners may not have heard it the first time, or understood it, or had time to write it down. Include examples or concrete ideas. These help both understanding and remembering. Use short sentences.

- ***Stress Important Points.*** This can be done with your tone of voice. It can also be done explicitly, e.g., "Write this down"; "This is important"; "This will be on the test."

- ***Pause.*** Give your listeners time to think, and to write.

- ***Change Activities Frequently.*** The average adult attention span is 15 to 20 minutes, so change activities several times in a class. Many activities provide a change of pace: stop and ask questions; have your students discuss a point with one or several others, and then get several groups to report to the whole class; have them write for a few minutes; or have them work a practice problem using a method you have presented in your lecture. By adding a "change up" to your lecture, you can revitalize your students' attention and thus give them renewed attention several times in one meeting, rather than just at the beginning.

Questioning in the Classroom

How to Ask Questions

Information; and to use the public speaking opportunity to motivate students.

By learning how to use questions effectively in the classroom, instructors can accomplish a number of interrelated goals. First, by engaging students in a question and answer dialogue, the usual "one-way" flow of information from instructor to students is transformed into a more interactive process. Students become more active participants in their own learning. In addition, skillful questioning can encourage students to engage in higher-level cognitive processes (analysis, synthesis, and evaluation), thus helping to develop their capacity for critical thinking. The current literature suggests several tactics that may assist teachers in improving the use of questioning in their teaching.

- After asking a question, wait for a response. Do not answer the question yourself; don't repeat it, rephrase it, modify it, call on another student to answer it, or replace it with another question until you have waited at least three to five seconds. Studies show that the average "wait time" is as low as 0.9 seconds, which is clearly not long enough. Students need time to think about the question. With and prepare their responses time of three to five seconds, students respond more, use complex cognitive processes, and begin to ask more questions.

- Ask only one question at a time. Do not ask a string of questions one after the other in the same utterance. For example, ask, "Compare the skeleton of an ape with that of a human." Do not ask, "How are apes and humans alike? Are they alike in bone structure and/or family structure and/or places where they live?" A series of questions tends to confuse students. They are not able to determine just what the teacher is requesting from them. Napell (1978) states that videotape replays reveal an interesting pattern when the teacher asks a series of questions. "Hands will go up in response to the first question, and a few will go down during the second, and those hands remaining up will gradually get lower and lower as the instructor finally concludes with a question very different from the one for which the hands were initially raised."

- Collect several answers to your question, even if the first student to answer gives a perfect response. Not all students think at the same speed, and you want to encourage those who were not first to continue reflecting. Often, the third or fourth answers will add dimensions that the first answer missed.

- When student questions are desired, request them explicitly, wait, and then acknowledge student contributions. For example, a teacher may wish to solicit questions about the plays of Shakespeare, which the class has been studying. The instructor might say, "What questions or clarifications of points need to be raised?" or, "Please ask questions about the main characters or the minor characters, whichever you wish at this point," or "In light of Sally's allusion to Lady Macbeth, I invite you to ask her some questions for embellishment or clarification." Avoid soliciting questions without a context, as in the classic, "Any questions?"

- Indicate to students that questions are not a sign of stupidity but rather the manifestation of concern and thought about the topic. Be very careful not to subtly or even jokingly convey the message that a student is stupid for asking for a clarification or restatement of an idea already raised in class or in the text.

- Let students try out their answers by quickly discussing them in pairs or by writing for a minute or two. They are much more willing to share their answers with the class when they have had this opportunity.

- Use a variety of probing and explaining questions. Ask questions that require different approaches to the topic, such as causal, teleological, functional, or chronological explanations. Avoid beginning your question with the words "why" and "explain," and instead phrase your questions with words which give stronger clues about the type of explanation sought. Thus, for a chronological explanation, instead of asking, "Why did we have a depression in the 1930s?" try "What series of events led up to the stock market crash of 1929 and the high unemployment in the 1930s?"

Answering Students' Questions

When answering a student's question, keep in mind your goals for that day's class. If the question moves the class toward that goal, you will want to give a complete answer or to redirect it to the class for discussion. If the question is not pertinent, you can tell the student where he or she can find an answer or offer to discuss it after class.

New instructors are often at a loss when they do not know the answer to a question. But it is not necessary to be able to field every question, and students can sense when an instructor "fakes" an answer. Instead, the instructor can offer to find the answer (and then should be sure and follow up) or suggest to the student where he or she can find the answer to the question.

In responding to student questions, a number of guidelines can positively reinforce good student responses and facilitate further discussion.

- Praise the student in a strong, positive way for a correct or positive response. Use such terms as "excellent answer," "absolutely correct," and "bull's eye." These terms are quite different from the common mild phrases teachers often use such as "O.K.," "hmm hum," and "all right." Especially when the response is long, the teacher should try to find at least some part that deserves praise and then comment on it.

- Comment specifically about that student's response. Tell the student why it is a good answer. For example, suppose that a student has offered an excellent response to the question, "What function did the invasion of the Kuwait serve for Iraq?" The instructor might say, "That was excellent, Pat. You included national political reasons as well as mentioning the Iraqi drive to become a pan-Arabic leader." This response gives an excellent rating to the student in an explicit and strong form. It also demonstrates that the instructor has listened carefully to the student's ideas.

- Build on the student's response. If the instructor continues to discuss a point after a student response, he or she should try to incorporate the key elements of the response into the discussion. If you do not acknowledge that this is the student's point, you risk being seen as "co-opting" the student's answer. By acknowledging the student's response, the teacher shows that he or she values the points made. By referring to the student explicitly by name (e.g., "As Pat pointed out, Kuwait's political status . . .") the teacher gives credit where credit is due.

- Avoid the "Yes, but . . ." reaction. Teachers use "Yes, but . . ." or its equivalent when a response is wrong or at least partly wrong. The overall impact of these phrases is negative and deceptive even though the teacher's intent is probably positive. The "Yes, but . . ." fielding move says that the response is correct or appropriate with one breath and then takes away the praise with the next. Some straightforward are:

  1. Wait to at least a count of five with the expectation that another student will volunteer a correct or better response.

  2. Ask, "How did you arrive at that response?" (Be careful, though, not to ask this question only

when you receive inadequate responses, ask it also at times when you receive a perfectly good response).

3. Say, "You're right regarding X and that's great; wrong regarding Y. Now we need to correct Y so we can get everything correct."

4. Say, "Thanks. Is there someone who wants to respond to the question or comment on the response we've already heard?"

5. These four alternatives are obviously not adequate to fit all cases. Indeed, it is generally difficult to field wrong or partially wrong responses because students are sensitive to teacher criticism. However, with these alternatives as examples, you will probably be able to generate others as needed.

Teaching Outside Your Field of Specialization

If you are assigned to teach outside of your speciality, you'll have to work to stay at least a week ahead of your brightest students. Remember that you are not responsible for knowing all the answers; don't feel compelled to apologize for your "lack of knowledge." If you cannot answer a question or you have made an error, admit it, but tell your students where they may find the answer or offer to look it up . . . and then do it. (This is good advice for teaching within your own field as well.) University students are usually

Extension Methods

In the previous chapter, the mass communication methods that the extension agent can employ in his work with farmers were reviewed. In this chapter, two other extension methods that the agent can employ will be examined. They are (a) the individual method, in which the agent deals with farmers on a one-to-one basis; and (b) the group method, in which the agent brings the farmers together in one form or another in order to undertake his extension work. Each of these methods demands different approaches and techniques on the part of the agent, and these will be examined later.

The two methods are suited to different purposes. It is important for the extension agent to consider the range of individual and group methods at his disposal and to select the method appropriate to the situation. It is also important to remember the educational purpose of extension work, and to ensure that the method selected is used to promote the farmers' better understanding of the technology involved. Both individual and group extension methods involve the agent in a face-to-face relationship with the farmer, and this relationship should be one of mutual confidence and respect. The agent, therefore, must think carefully about his use of individual or group extension methods and ensure that his relationship with the farmer is sensitively developed.

Three different extension methods: mass, group and individual

Individual Methods of Extension

Individual or face-to-face methods are probably the most universally used extension methods in both developed and developing countries. The extension agent meets the farmer at home or on the farm and discusses issues of mutual interest, giving the farmer both information and advice. The atmosphere of the meeting is usually informal and relaxed, and the farmer is able to benefit from the agent's individual attention. Individual meetings are probably the most important aspect of all extension work and invaluable for building confidence between the agent and the farmer.

Learning is very much an individual process and, although group methods enable the agent to reach a greater number of farmers, personal contact with and the individual attention of the extension agent are important supports for a farmer. The personal influence of the extension worker can be a critical factor in helping a farmer through difficult decisions, and can also be instrumental in getting the farmer to participate in extension activities. A farmer is often likely to listen to the advice given by the extension agent and will be grateful for this individual attention.

This individual contact between the extension agent and the farmer can take a number of forms, each of which will be considered below.

Farm Visits

Farm visits are the most common form of personal contact between the agent and the farmer and often constitute over 50 per cent of the agent's extension activities. Because they take up so much of the agent's time, it is important to be clear about the purpose of such visits and to plan them carefully.

Farm visits can:

- Familiarize the extension agent with the farmer and his family;
- Enable him to give specific advice or information to the farmer;
- Build up the agent's knowledge of the area, and of the kinds of problems which farmers face;
- Permit him to explain a new recommended practice or follow up and observe results to date;
- Arouse general interest among the farmers and stimulate their involvement in extension activities.

At times, the extension agent will make a farm visit spontaneously if he happens to be passing by and it is convenient to drop in. Such informal visits may have no specific purpose but are a useful way of maintaining contact and gradually building links with farmers. Even if the agent just drops in to greet the farmer and his family, this short visit can do a lot to foster mutual respect and friendship. Usually, however, farm visits will be part of the agent's general plan of work and will be programmed into his monthly schedule of activities.

Planning the Visit

First, it is important to be very clear about the purpose of the visit. Before a visit, the extension agent should review the file on the farm to be visited and consult any other information available on the farmer. He must be fully informed on the relevant details of the farm he is visiting and should summarize the situation in a few notes before setting off. He must try to avoid showing ignorance of the farmer and his farming activities, or the need to consult his file during the visit.

In addition, the visit should be planned to fit in with other local extension activities. For example, if a demonstration or meeting is planned for the morning, then it may be possible to programme a number of individual farm visits for the afternoon. Whenever possible, the agent should make an appointment at a time convenient to the farmer, to ensure that the farmer will be there and that the journey will not be wasted. If an appointment is made in advance, the farmer will also have time to prepare for the visit and to think about the issues to be discussed with the agent.

Checklist

- Make an appointment if possible.
- Decide the purpose of the visit.
- Review previous records and information.

- Prepare specialist subject matter that might be required.
- Schedule the visit into the overall work plan.

Making the Visit

The agent must always remember the basic educational purpose of extension and his role in this process. The agent's role is not just one of transmitting new knowledge or recommendations; he must also devote time during visits to building up the farmer's confidence and interest. One of the first points to think about when making a farm visit is how to start a conversation. The first few minutes of contact are extremely important for establishing a good relationship, particularly if it is the first meeting. Methods of establishing rapport and of initiating conversation differ from culture to culture. Small talk in order to break the ice is often an important first step, and gives both sides a chance to relax and to get to know each other a little before more serious matters are discussed. Time must be spent in greeting the farmer and his family and an informal chat will not be wasted. Similarly, local customs should be followed as regards accepting hospitality. If visitors are expected to drink tea or coffee with the host, then the agent should do so, while taking care not to acquire a reputation of one who spends all his time drinking tea or coffee during visits.

The agent should then choose the moment when more formal business can be discussed. The choice of the discussion topic is also an important decision for the extension worker. If he is sensitive to the farmer's needs, he will discuss matters relevant to these needs. Moreover, he will discuss these topics at the farmer's level and in language that the farmer is accustomed to use. In this respect, the agent should be a good listener as well as a good talker, and he should encourage farmers to explain and discuss issues at their own pace and in their own words. It is important for the agent to find a reason to praise farmers for some aspect of farm management in order to encourage their involvement and make then feel that they also have knowledge to contribute.

The visit may cover a whole range of activities. The farmer may need further explanation or information about a particular new practice and it may be necessary to demonstrate this. If further technical information is required, this can be noted and, at a later date, an appropriate information bulletin can be sent. The agent may also brief the farmer generally on government agricultural policy, or describe the range of extension activities in the area and encourage the farmer to get involved. Some visits may also be of an emergency nature when the agent will be expected to give on-the-spot advice concerning a particular problem. Finally, the agent should always be alert during farm visits for ways to promote the involvement of other family members, including spouses and young people, in other local extension activities such as a youth club or a food preparation demonstration.

If possible, it is useful to set up a system to keep a record of the content of farm visits; this could be simply a notebook in which the essential details of each visit (date, purpose, problems, decisions, etc.) are recorded. Such a farm record system is very useful in helping the agent to keep a more detailed account of each visit and it is invaluable when a new agent is taking over. The records are also very useful in evaluating farmers' progress.

Checklist

- Be punctual for the visit.
- Greet the farmer and this family.
- Praise the farmer's work.
- Encourage the farmer to explain and discuss any problems.

- Provide any technical or other information required.
- Record the details of the visit.
- Plan with the far recording and follow-up

The purpose of any farm visit will be lost if its content and conclusion are not recorded and no follow-up action taken. During the visit, the agent will almost certainly make a series of notes and observations. On the first available office day, these notes should be neatly transcribed on an individual card kept at the extension office. After each visit, the agent should record the date, the purpose, the conclusions or recommendations arising from the visit, as well as any other additional information or observations which he feels will be helpful. The agent must not store this information in his head, since, if he is transferred, the incoming agent will be left with a gap in information and will find it difficult to catch up with the situation.

Finally, the agent should arrange for any follow-up that may have been agreed with the farmer. This could involve the sending of further specialist information, or arranging for a specialist colleague to visit the farmer concerned. Whatever the case, it is vitally important that the agent follow-up on any issues or problems that he was not able to deal with in person. Failure to do so will disappoint the farmer and lessen his confidence in the agent. It is very important to maintain the confidence and trust that can often take years to build up. He should also schedule his next visit to the farmer in his work programme.

Checklist

Record purpose of and decision resulting from visit. Arrange for any follow-up information or advice to be sent. Schedule the next visit to the farmer.

Farm visits are perhaps the single most important aspect of the agent's work in terms of establishing rapport with the farmers in his area and of building the trust and confidence that are vital to the success of his work. However, farm visits take up a lot of time and only a few farmers can be reached. Farm visits are, therefore, a costly extension method and for this reason they must be carefully thought out and planned. The visits must make an impact and must lead to positive agricultural development if they are to justify their cost. Finally, the agent should beware of visiting some farmers repeatedly. This would not only severely limit the range of his activities, but could also arouse the resentment of other farmers who might feel excluded.

Office Calls

Just as the extension agent visits the farmer, so he can expect that from time to time the farmer will visit him at his office. Such a visit is often a reflection of the interest which the agent may have aroused among the local farmers. The more confidence local farmers have in the extension agent, the more likely they are to visit him. Such office visits are less time consuming for the extension worker, and offer some of the advantages of a farm visit. While no extension agent would wish to be overwhelmed by such visits every day, he should encourage farmers to drop in if it is convenient for them to make the exchange of visits two-way.

As with farm visits, office visits similarly have to be prepared. Although the agent may not know when a farmer is likely to drop in, he can at least arrange the extension office in such a way that the visitor feels at ease and can understand the activities of the office. The arrangement could include:

- Ensuring that access to the extension office is adequately posted and the agent's name displayed;
- Having a notice-board clearly displayed upon which useful, up-to-date information can be pinned;

- Having one or two chairs where visitors can wait for appointments;
- Displaying any bulletins, circulars or other written extension literature that the visitor can read.

For some farmers, a visit to the extension office may be a difficult experience. The agent should, therefore, try to put the farmer at ease, asking a few questions in order to get the farmer to explain his problems. The agent should be polite but purposeful, and try to find out the reason for the visit as quickly as possible. When he feels that the matter has been adequately discussed, the agent should tactfully terminate the interview in order not to let it drift aimlessly on. The agent should always escort the visitor out, and say goodbye. A note on these office visits should also be added to the farmer's record card, and any follow-up implemented.

Letters

Occasionally, the extension agent will correspond with a farmer by letter. Letters can be a follow-up inquiry resulting from an agent's farm visit, or sent because a farmer is unable to make a personal office visit. Drafting and replying to letters are very important skills for the extension worker and he should give every thought to them. Problems can arise with the use of words or complex technological language, or if the letter has been badly typed or written. In writing a letter to a farmer, the extension agent should try to put himself in the farmer's shoes. The letter should be in the local language, preferably not on impressively headed writing-paper, and should always contain some personal greeting to the farmer. Often, farmers will show such letters to their neighbours and thus it is important to create a favorable impression. The following points are important:

- Letters should be clear and concise, so as not to confuse the reader;

- The information in the letter should be complete and relevant to the issues raised;
- Where possible, letters should be answered promptly. If time is needed to collect information for the reply, a short letter of acknowledgement should be sent;
- A copy of the letter must always be made and entered in the office file.

Individual Methods

Telephone Calls

Telephone calls and office visits serve a very similar purpose. It is improbable that the extension worker will deal with many of the farmers in his area (if at all) by telephone. If the telephone is used, however, it will not be for long discussion but for passing on specific advice or information. Whatever the reason, it is important for the agent to speak clearly, to note the main points discussed and to enter them on the farmer's record.

Informal Contacts

Informal contacts will occur continually during the agent's stay in a particular area. Market days, holiday celebrations or religious events will bring him into contact with the farmers with whom he is working who will inevitably talk about their problems. By attending such events, the agent can become well acquainted with the area where he works and with the farmers and their problems, and he will be able to pass on ideas and information on an informal basis.

Group Methods of Extension

The extension agent should consider the use of the group approach in his work with farmers. The use of groups in extension has become more common over the past decade, and indeed a number of new ideas have emerged about how groups may be used most effectively. For example, the widespread Small Farmer Development Programme (SFDP) in Southeast Asia was based upon group methods and it has produced two manuals which detail the approach of group extension work. Furthermore, in Latin America, work with extension groups in Brazil and Colombia has shown the usefulness to extension of the formation of extension groups, and how these groups can support extension activity.

Advantages of Group Methods

It has been seen that individual extension methods can be costly in both terms of time and scarce extension resources, and that they reach only a limited number of people. There is also the danger that too much emphasis upon individuals can lead to undue concentration on progressive farmers to the detriment of the poorer farmers.

Coverage

The group method offers the possibility of greater extension coverage, and is therefore more cost-effective. Using the group method, the extension worker can reach more farmers and in this way make contact with many more farmers who have had no previous contact with extension activities.

Learning Environment

Extension groups offer a more reflective learning environment in which the farmer can listen, discuss and decide upon his involvement in the extension activity. The support of the group helps an individual farmer to make decisions and determine a course of action. The group creates a supportive atmosphere, and individual farmers can gain greater self-confidence by joining others to discuss new ideas and try out new practices.

Action

The group method brings together farmers with similar problems. Often, these problems demand concerted action (tackling the erosion of a hillside, for example), and such action can be taken more effectively by a group rather than by an individual, who may be overwhelmed by the enormity of certain problems.

Important Issues in Group Extension

Before considering in detail a number of different group methods of extension, it is necessary to look at some of the more important issues concerning the extension group. To form, structure and develop a group of farmers for extension purposes is a complex process, and such groups do not appear overnight. It is not sufficient for the extension agent merely to bring the farmers together for a particular activity. He must give time and thought to the fact that the farmers will constitute a group, will function as a group and will display characteristics associated with groups. Experience in different parts of the world has shown that there are four sets of important issues that the agent will have to bear in mind:

Purpose

The agent should be aware of two main purposes in his work with groups. First, he should try to develop the group, to encourage its members to continue to meet and to establish the group on a permanent basis. In this way, the agent will be developing a base from which group members can continue their development efforts. Second, the agent should use the group to transmit new ideas, information and knowledge that will assist the farmers in their agricultural activities. While the second use of groups is more common, it is important that the agent consider the initial development of the group as an equally vital extension activity.

Size

The most suitable size for groups in rural extension is between 20 and 40 members. If the group is too large, it becomes unwieldy and many farmers may feel lost and bewildered. Smaller groups allow closer contact, a better chance of involvement and more opportunity for strengthening bonds of friendship and support among members. One common determinant of group size is geographical location: its membership will be restricted to those living within a particular area.

Membership

Since the extension agent's job is to help farmers identify and tackle problems, it is better to have groups of farmers with common problems. If the agent is working with a group made up of different types of farmers, ranging, for example, from big landowners to small, tenant farmers, it may be difficult for him to achieve a common purpose within the group. The agent, therefore, should pay careful attention to group membership and try to ensure that its members share a common interest and problems.

Agent's Relationship with Group

The agent should give considerable thought to his relationship with the group. Ideally, he will want to encourage the group's formation and help to strengthen it. If his extension work takes him to another area, it is hoped that he will leave behind a structure that can function with a minimum of extension support. The agent should try to avoid being directly responsible for setting up the groups and should try to ensure that they are based, where possible, upon existing social or cultural community groups. In all of his activities with groups, the agent should beware of the group becoming too dependent upon him and of creating a structure that needs him for survival. Instead, the agent should strive to encourage an element of independence in the group, by encouraging the group to take the initiative in extension activities and to decide for itself in what way the agent can be of assistance.

These four issues, then, should be borne in mind by the agent as he pursues his work with extension groups. His main concern will be to do his work well and to ensure that, through the group approach, more farmers come into contact with new ideas and practices. In the long run, group work might be even more productive and effective if he gave some thought to the development of the group itself in his extension work.

Types of Group Extension Methods

Group Meetings

Calling the members of a group or the inhabitants of a local community together for a meeting is the commonest group extension method. Although there may be an air of informality about such meetings, they will nevertheless need to be carefully thought out and planned. The group or community meeting is a useful educational forum where the agent and farmers can come together, and ideas can be openly discussed and analyzed. The agent will probably have information about a new government policy, or agricultural idea or practice. He will want to introduce this new information, to seek the opinions of community members and gain their support for extension activities. Indeed, there are a whole range of purposes for such community or group meetings:

Information Meetings. The agent calls the group or community together to communicate a specific piece of new information which he feels will benefit them and upon which he seeks their advice.

Planning Meetings. The main purpose is to review a particular problem, suggest a number of solutions and decide upon a course of action.

Special Interest Meetings. Topics of specific interest to a particular group of people (e.g., horticulture, bee keeping, or dairy farming) are presented and discussed in detail at a level relevant to those participating.

General Community Meetings. Men, women and young people of a community are invited to attend to discuss issues of general community interest. It is important to hold such general meetings occasionally so as to avoid any community group feeling that it is excluded from extension activities.

Whatever the case, however, the agent should only call a meeting if he thinks that it can be useful. If farmers feel that their time has been wasted in coming to a meeting, they may refuse to come to subsequent meetings and thus frustrate the agent's work. Once he decides to hold a meeting, the agent should make careful preparations and check a number of important arrangements which will be necessary to ensure a successful meeting.

The basic purpose of the meeting should be agreed and to determine this the agent should consult community or group leaders. Only then can the agent and community leaders consider the content and the best approach to the meeting. It may be useful to write down in a few words what the purpose is, and then to see what are the important aspects to be considered. If it is to be a meeting for providing information, the agent must structure his material in a coherent form and decide in what sequence he is going to present it. If it is to be a general community meeting, then, similarly, he must decide how he will structure the meeting and introduce discussion on the issues he has in mind.

Form of the Meeting

Depending upon the nature and purpose of the meeting, the agent must decide the most appropriate form for the meeting and how it can best be conducted. The agent should consider the appropriateness of the different forms the meeting could take and, in consultation with community members, decide accordingly. Ideally, the ingredients should be mixed to suit the occasion.

Smaller meetings are more likely to meet the specific needs of those who attend. When plans are to be made or decisions taken, a small number of representatives will usually achieve more than a large gathering of all community members. On other occasions, it will be important for the meeting to be open to as many people as possible.

A formal meeting, with chairman, agenda and written record of proceedings, is appropriate when specific business has to be dealt with or decisions reached. The chairman keeps the meeting to the central issues, and the decisions of the meeting are recorded accurately so that they cannot be disputed later. In an informal meeting, people feel more able to express their own point of view and less dominated by the structure and formality of the proceedings. However, an open, unstructured discussion, although it allows all to participate, may result in a few people dominating the proceedings.

A lecture or talk allows the agent (or other speaker) to convey a detailed, well-prepared message to his audience on a specific issue; for example, a new piece of technology can be presented in this way, and illustrated by visual aids. It should be remembered, however, that the lecture is a particularly tedious approach to meetings and care must be taken to ensure that people will not get bored. Alternatively, in a discussion, many people are able to express points of view and ask questions. Discussions may be completely open and unstructured, or based on a prepared agenda of discussion points.

Planning the Meeting

There are two important decisions to make regarding the time and location. A date and time for the meeting must be decided and announced. The time should be convenient to all concerned and should avoid clashes with other events or activities. The meeting-place should be well-known, easy to get to and appropriate for the form of meeting. The meeting-place should also be comfortable and have the facilities necessary for the meeting. An extension agent would never hold a meeting at midday, on a very hot day, in the open sun. Such a meeting could be disastrous, as well as cause considerable discomfort.

After the above two issues have been considered, it may be useful for the agent to draw up a list of other arrangements to be made in preparation for the meeting. Such a checklist could include:

Checklist

- Publicity for the meeting
- Seating arrangements
- Audio-visual equipment and material, or other educational aids
- Agenda, and order of events
- Guest speakers or other specialists who will contribute to the meeting
- Chairman to take charge of the meeting, who should be elected by the community
- Refreshments for speakers and, where necessary, other participants.

Conducting the Meeting

Even the most carefully prepared meeting can fail if it is not conducted in the right manner. While the above arrangements are important, the way the actual meeting proceeds will determine whether it will be a success or not.

The agent must be conscious that he is dealing with adults who do not want to sit for hours listening to a speaker talk endlessly. The agent should try to vary the agenda of the meeting: for example, a short talk, accompanied by visual aids, followed by comments and questions.

Variety of content, as well as a chance for the farmers to participate, will be important. In addition, the meeting must not go on too long. One-and-a-half hours are probably sufficient for a group or community meeting. It is better to have a highly productive, short meeting than one which rambles on and loses effect.

The agent's role in the meeting should also respond to the circumstances. He should encourage the community to appoint a chairman and should allow the chairman to conduct business. The agent's role should basically be to inform and support, and he should not dominate the meeting. Furthermore, the meeting should not resemble a classroom with the agent as teacher and the farmers as pupils. The agent should make every effort to ensure that during the proceedings the community members feel that it is their meeting and that they have a part to play.

As a guide to the proceedings of the meeting, the agent should keep the following points in mind. He should start the meeting on time. Then he should welcome community members and special guests, explain the purpose of the meeting and the programme to be followed, and begin the programme. Later, the agent should encourage questions and discussion, and be prepared to summarize the main points and note important decisions. The meeting should be closed with thanks to all concerned.

As the most commonly used form of group extension method, the group or community meeting will be most effective if carefully thought out and planned. After each meeting, the agent should make a brief record of the proceedings and the principal decisions taken. He should also take any prompt follow-up action that has been decided.

Demonstrations

Farmers like to see how a new idea works, and also what effect it can have on increasing their crop production. Both purposes can be achieved by means of a farm demonstration. A good, practical demonstration is an invaluable method in extension work. The demonstration is a particularly powerful method to use with farmers who do not read easily. A demonstration will give such farmers the opportunity to observe, at first hand, the differences between a recommended new crop practice and traditional practices. The strength of the demonstration should lie in its simplicity and its ability to present the farmers with concrete results.

There are two principal types of demonstration used by extension agents—method demonstration and result demonstration.

Method Demonstration

Method demonstrations basically show farmers how to do something. In the method demonstration, the farmer is shown step by step how, for example, to plant seeds in line, to use a mechanical duster to control insects, or to top tobacco. The agent will probably be dealing with farmers who have already accepted the particular practice being demonstrated, but who now want to know how to do it themselves.

The main advantage of the method demonstration is that the extension agent can explain simple farming skills to a large number of people, thus increasing the impact of his extension work. Moreover, as farmers are able to participate, there is a greater chance that they will benefit from the demonstration than if they were passively hearing it in a lecture.

The main limitation of a method demonstration is that, if there are too many farmers present, only a few get a chance to see, hear and do. The agent must be conscious that the demonstration is a learning experience and prepare the event accordingly. It is also vital that the demonstration be well thought out and competently conducted.

Result Demonstration

The main purpose of a result demonstration is to show local farmers that a particular new recommendation is practicable under local conditions. Comparison is the important element in a result demonstration: comparison between compost and no compost, between poor seed and selected seed, or between use of fertilizer and no fertilizer. "Seeing is believing" is an age-old expression, but one appropriate to a result demonstration. Until a farmer has actually seen the results of, for example, the application of a fertilizer, he will not be convinced by the agent's recommendation. By showing tangible results of a new practice recommended by the extension service, the agent can help to create confidence among the farmers and can greatly encourage them to try the practice themselves.

A result demonstration is an ideal way to present to farmers a comparison between traditional and new practices. It can also help to establish confidence in more scientific farming methods and increase the farmers' confidence in ideas originating from research stations. It shows proof of the value of a new practice. A result demonstration is also a useful tool that an agent can use to establish confidence among farmers in a new area.

Its major limitation is that it takes a long time to mature and is thus a costly use of extension resources. If, in the end, for whatever reason, the new practice should fail, it could have disastrous consequences. Often such failures (for example, because of lack of rain) are outside the control of the agent.

Both method and result demonstrations are extension activities that require a lot of thought, careful planning and efficient execution. Although the two demonstrations differ somewhat in their purposes, they share a lot of common points and, in terms of their preparation and execution, they can be considered together.

Basic Principles for Demonstrations

Before the agent begins to plan and prepare for a demonstration, he should be clear about a number of key points that will guide his preparation and handling of the demonstration.

Participation. Where possible, demonstrations should be carried out on local farms with farmers' participation rather than on an extension plot or research station. Farmers will have more confidence if a demonstration is held on a neighbour's land, or if a new practice is shown by a fellow farmer, than if it is carried out by agents on extension land. The more the local farmers can be involved in the whole process of a demonstration, the greater will be their self-confidence and readiness to learn.

Simplicity. Simple, clear-cut demonstrations of a single practice or new idea will be far more effective than ambitious and over-complex demonstrations that demand too much of the farmer. It is better to proceed step by step with a number of demonstrations than to try do to everything at once.

Learning. The demonstration is a learning environment and should be run in such a way that the farmers do in fact learn something. A demonstration is a type of classroom, and the agent must be conscious of classroom requirements in terms of space, time, equipment and the teaching method to use.

Preparation. An extension agent should never contemplate holding a demonstration without careful planning and preparation. A demonstration hastily given could have disastrous consequences.

Planning the Demonstration

When the agent decides that a demonstration would be useful at a particular time, he must then dedicate some time to planning and preparing for it. In this respect, he must ask himself a number of questions.

- What is the objective of the demonstration?
- Why is the demonstration the most suitable extension method, and what would be the usefulness of the new idea to be demonstrated?
- When should the demonstration be held? When is the most convenient date and time both for the farmers and in terms of the application of the new idea?
- Where is the demonstration to be held? Which suitable location is the most convenient for the farmers.

The agent should work out in some detail his answers to the above questions before proceeding any further. It is very important that the reasons for the demonstration be appropriate and clearly understood and that there is a realistic expectation that the demonstration will be of benefit to the farmers involved.

Preparing the Demonstration

The more carefully the agent can prepare all the details of the demonstration, the more chance he will have of it running smoothly. The following are the key areas of preparation.

- Consult the local people and seek their help and advice in the preparation of the demonstration.
- Prepare a detailed plan of the demonstration, the main issues to be covered, the sequence of events,

the resources needed and the contributions required from other people.

- Collect information and material available on the new idea or practice to be demonstrated, and make sure that the topic is familiar and that questions can be answered.

- Check that all the support material is ready (e.g., audio-visual aids, implements).

- Select those farmers who will take part in the demonstration and brief them on the outline of events.

- Ensure that the demonstration has been publicized and that the farmers know exactly when and where it is to take place.

- Visit the demonstration site beforehand to make sure that all is in order and that the site is appropriate.

Supervising the Demonstration

During the demonstration, the agent's role should be to supervise but not to dominate. He should actively support the farmer who may be assisting in the demonstration, and encourage the others to participate as much as they can. The agent should be keen to ensure that all those present benefit from the demonstration. During the demonstration, therefore, the agent should:

Welcome the participants, make them feel at ease and ensure that they have all they require to benefit fully from the demonstration.

Explain the purpose of the demonstration, what it is hoped to achieve and what the various stages are that will be followed. Distribute any literature or other material which may have been prepared as a guide for the participants. Conduct the demonstration in person or be ready to help the demonstrator farmer. Proceed at a pace the farmers can follow, and be prepared to explain again or answer questions from participants. Emphasize key points and explain the practice step by step in simple words. In a method demonstration, ensure that all those who wish to do so have a chance to practice the demonstration themselves.

Summarize the main issues or points which have arisen, encourage questions from the farmers and make sure that the participants have had every opportunity to try out or examine the practice being demonstrated. Conclude the demonstration with a vote of thanks to all concerned, and with a few comments about any follow-up activities planned.

Follow-up

It is important that any interest generated by, or decisions taken at, the demonstration be followed up. Farmers will feel let down if the agent does not do so. This follow-up will be useful for the agent as well. Demonstrations can often result in good contacts with local farmers, and the agent may be able to enlist their support for future activities. It is also important that the agent reflect upon the demonstration and evaluate its effectiveness. The agent should, therefore, write a report and prepare a record of the demonstration, noting the names of the participants, the effect achieved and personal impressions of the usefulness of the field days.

Field Days

Field days are usually opportunities to hold method or result demonstrations on a slightly larger scale, and are usually run in a more informal and less highly structured manner. The purpose is often to introduce a new idea and a new crop, and to stimulate the interest of as many farmers as possible. Experimental stations or other government centres may be used for field days, but it is more usual and profitable for them to be held on the land of a local farmer. There is a greater chance of making an impact if the field day is held on a farmer's land, and if the farmer plays a part in running it and explaining the purpose.

Field days can range in size from a small group to annual events attracting hundreds of farmers. Since the aim is a general introduction to some new idea, there is less need to be concerned about limiting the numbers. The extension agent's role on the field day is to support the farmer on whose land it is being held, to offer general guidance to ensure that things run smoothly and to be available to answer questions and queries.

It is probably better not to over organize the field day but to try to create an atmosphere in which visiting farmers can inspect, inquire, question and generally get to know what is available.

Although the agent will try to encourage an open and informal atmosphere for the field day, there is still a considerable amount of preparation needed to ensure that it runs well. The issues which the agent must consider are very similar to those noted under demonstrations and will not be repeated here. It may be useful, however, to bear a few additional points in mind.

Limit the numbers to the capacity of the field, to avoid overcrowding. Ensure a good layout of field-day activities, with easy access and facility of movement around the field. Encourage the demonstrator farmer to take most of the initiative; give him support but do not take over the field day from him. Provide suitably large visual material and also, if necessary, a loudspeaker, to ensure that all can hear. Check that extension literature and other material are available for consultation.

Conclude the field day by bringing all the participants together, reviewing the day's proceedings and the main items seen and discussed, and explain any future relevant extension activities.

A field day is a day out for farmers and is often a welcome relief from their daily hard work. The agent should, therefore, provide an interesting and well-presented exhibition, suitable refreshments and points of rest, and generally create an atmosphere in which the farmers will feel at ease and will be eager to know what is going on.

Tours

Farmers like to visit farms in other districts to see how they work, what they grow and what kinds of problems the farmers there are facing. A tour is a series of field demonstrations on different farms, or at different centre, and can often attract a lot of interest from local farmers. The tour should give local farmers a chance to see how other farmers cultivate their land, and to exchange ideas and experiences with them. It is important, therefore, that the area to be visited be in some way similar agriculturally to that of the visiting farmers.

As with all other forms of extension, tours have to be well thought out, planned, prepared and conducted. The five stages of determining the objective, planning the content, preparing the arrangements, conducting the tour and arranging for appropriate follow-up will be a guide to the extension agent. However, it may be useful to add these points:

Visit the area first to become familiar with local conditions, the farms to be visited, the route and road conditions.

Limit the tour to what is possible. It is better to do a short tour in which visitors can have a good look at local farms than to arrange an ambitious tour and be pushed for time. Don't tire the visitors out. Encourage the host farmers to do all the explaining and to take charge of the tour.

Arrange for food and drink during the tour.

Conclude the tour with a short summary of the main events and note any comments or conclusions.

A field tour is an ideal method of involving farmers and of stimulating genuine interest in extension activities. It is also very useful in bringing farmers together to discuss common problems, and to gain useful experience of other areas.

Provide suitably large visual material and also, if necessary, a loudspeaker, to ensure that all can hear. Check that extension literature and other material are available for consultation.

Conclude the field day by bringing all the participants together, reviewing the day's proceedings and the main items seen and discussed, and explain any future relevant extension activities.

A field day is a day out for farmers and is often a welcome relief from their daily hard work. The agent should, therefore, provide an interesting and well-presented exhibition, suitable refreshments and points of rest, and generally create an atmosphere in which the farmers will feel at ease and will be eager to know what is going on.

Public Speaking

Public speaking is a skill which the agent will be called upon to practice frequently. A principal task of the agent is communication; this inevitably involves public speaking to explain a new idea, conduct a demonstration or generally take part in a community discussion.

Speaking in public is a very useful and effective form of communication, if done competently. A public speech gives the extension agent an opportunity to demonstrate his enthusiasm and technical knowledge. Some people are natural public speakers and easily and competently arrange their material and present it in a way which is both interesting and intelligible to the audience. On the other hand, if an extension agent is poorly prepared to give his speech and delivers it badly in an uncomfortable situation, then his efforts could be counterproductive.

Public speaking represents an important aspect of an extension agent's work and one which he can use to great advantage if he prepares well. Most importantly, a talk must flow well and give the impression of being well-thoughtout. There is nothing mote off-putting for an audience than a speaker who fumbles his notes, forgets basic facts or talks too long. A well-prepared and delivered extension talk can make a considerable impression upon farmers and build up confidence in the extension agent.

While not all agents will have the same natural ability to speak publicly, there is much that an agent can do to improve his performance.

Public Speaking is an Important Part of Extension Work

Most agents will be able to develop a good approach to public speaking with application and practice. The points listed below are a useful guide to public speaking for the extension agent.

Preparation

As with all extension activities, the agent must prepare himself beforehand for a public speaking engagement, no matter how unimportant the event may seem. This preparation includes checking the facts, figures and other information to be included in the presentation, organizing the material in a logical manner and preparing any supporting audiovisual material. It is also useful to check the place where the talk is to be given and to take into consideration the interests, needs and knowledge of the expected audience.

Some agents find it useful to rehearse the talk beforehand, or at least the main points. The agent should not try to memorize the whole talk; instead, he should write the main items in order for reference in large print on paper or on small cards. Another technique is to note the main points on an overhead projector sheet which can be uncovered step by step as the speech progresses. This serves a dual purpose: helping the agent in the presentation and providing a summary of the main topics for the audience.

Content

Great care should be taken with the content of a talk, both in terms of the words and expressions used and also in the logical sequence of what is to be said. The subject of the talk should be introduced and a general outline of the subject given. The main body of the talk should contain the key points that the agent wishes to make. He should not put too much content into a talk; a short, concise and well-thoughtout talk will have far more effect than a lengthy, rambling presentation.

It is also important to take some care in the use of words and expressions and to adapt these, where possible, to the local context. Similarly, it is important to avoid the use of over-complex technical language or jargon, which might confuse the audience.

Mass Media in Extension

Mass media are those channels of communication which can expose large numbers of people to the same information at the same time. They include media which convey information by sound (radio, audio cassettes); moving pictures (television, film, video); and print (posters, newspapers, leaflets). The attraction of mass media to extension services is the high speed and low cost with which information can be communicated to people over a wide area. Although the cost of producing and transmitting a radio programme may seem high, when that cost is divided between the millions of people who may hear the programme, it is in fact a very cheap way of providing information. The cost of an hour's radio broadcast per farmer who listens can be less than one-hundredth of the cost of an hour's contact with an extension agent.

However, mass media cannot do all the jobs of an extension agent. They cannot offer personal advice and support, teach practical skills, or answer questions immediately. Their low cost suggests that they should be used for the tasks to which they are well suited. These include the following:

- Spreading awareness of new ideas and creating interest in farming innovations.

- Giving timely warnings about possible pest and disease outbreaks, and urgent advice on what action to take.

- Multiplying the impact of extension activities. A demonstration will only be attended by a small number of farmers, but the results will reach many more if they are reported in newspapers and on the radio.

- Sharing experiences with other individuals and communities. The success of a village in establishing a local tree plantation might stimulate other villages to do the same if it is broadcast over the radio. Farmers are also often interested in hearing about the problems of other farmers and how they have overcome them.

- Answering questions, and advising on problems common to a large number of farmers.

- Reinforcing or repeating information and advice. Information heard at a meeting or passed on by an extension agent can soon be forgotten. It will be remembered more easily if it is reinforced by mass media.

- Using a variety of sources that are credible to farmers. Instead of hearing advice from the extension agent only, through mass media farmers can be brought into contact with successful farmers from other areas, respected political figures and agricultural specialists.

Mass media communication requires specialist professional skills. Few extension agents will ever be required to produce radio programmes or to make films. However, extension agents can contribute to the successful use of mass media by providing material to media producers, in the form of newspaper stories, photographs, recorded interviews with farmers, items of information about extension activities or ideas for new extension films; and by using mass media in their extension work, for example, by distributing posters and leaflets or by encouraging farmers to listen to farm broadcasts.

Audio-visual Aids in Extension

The term audio-visual aid refers to anything that an extension agent uses to help to convey the message when communicating with farmers. The spoken word is the agent's main communication tool, but, whether the agent is speaking to a large village meeting or discussing a problem in a field with a group of farmers, its impact and effectiveness can be greatly increased by the use of suitable audio-visual aids. When selected and used properly, audio-visual aids can help in the following ways:

- The interest of the audience can be maintained if the agent varies the mode of presentation. It is difficult to concentrate for long on what someone is saying; but if the agent refers to a wall chart, or illustrates a point with some slides, his audience's attention can be maintained.

- When information is presented to more than one sense (sight and touch, for example, as well as hearing), more is taken in and it is better understood and remembered.

- Processes and concepts that are difficult to express in words alone can be explained. The procedure for applying for a loan, for example, may sound confusing, but a simple chart or diagram can make the process clearer. Again, the life cycle of a crop pest can be explained by showing a series of slides or drawings.

- The effects of decisions and actions that farmers might take can be shown. Photographs of a cattle dip or a model of a cooperative store can give farmers a clear idea of just what it is they might be considering.

- Pictures can have a more immediate impact on our emotions than words. Photographs of a heavy crop, for example, are likely to arouse interest more effectively than details of yields read out by an extension agent.

The Range of Audio-visual Aids

Extension agents often use sophisticated audio-visual aids which require electricity and complex machinery such as projectors or television sets. But there are many simple aids that the agent can make locally, and these have several advantages. They do not require a power source or heavy equipment, they do not cost much to produce and they can be made to suit the precise needs of the agent. Between these two extremes lies a wide range of more or less sophisticated aids. The distinction between a mass medium and an audio-visual aid lies only in the way it is used. All the mass media described earlier can be used as audio-visual aids. A film is a mass medium, in that it is shown to large audiences in many different places; but for an individual extension agent who uses it to increase the impact of a talk, it is an audio-visual aid. Many of the principles of media use discussed earlier also apply to audio-visual aids. The audio-visual aids available to the extension agent can now be examined.

Objects

A real object is often the most effective aid. It enables the audience to understand exactly what the extension agent is talking about. Equipment and tools can be shown, samples of diseased plants and insect pests displayed and different seed varieties and fertilizers handled by farmers.

Where an object is too large to be shown, a model of it can sometimes be used as a teaching aid. This applies particularly to buildings and other fixed structures. The construction of a poultry shed, for example, or the installation of a dip tank can be demonstrated by using a model, which can be taken to pieces in front of the audience.

Photographs offer another substitute for real objects. They can be passed around an audience or displayed by the agent. If a photograph is being taken to use as a visual aid, just the right amount of detail should be included for the audience to recognize it. Too much detail confuses and distracts, while too little prevents recognition. Photographs of people doing things are more likely to interest the audience than photographs of objects alone.

Chalkboards

Blackboards are widely available in schools, rural training institutes and extension offices. They may be fixed to an inside wall or supported on a freestanding easel which can be moved around. They are useful for setting down the main headings of a talk, for sketching simple drawings and diagrams, and for noting points raised in questions and discussion.

If using a blackboard, the agent should practice writing on it, if necessary by drawing horizontal chalk lines for guidance. He should make sure that the writing is large enough for someone at the back of the audience to see clearly and that the headings and phrases are kept short. There is not much space on blackboards and the agent will lose the audience's attention if he spends a lot of time with his back to them while writing.

Whiteboards have a smooth, shiny surface on which colored felt pens can be used, but it is important to use only pens with water-soluble ink. Whiteboards are easier to use than blackboards from both the agent's and the audience's point of view. The pens flow smoothly over the surface and the colours are much clearer than chalk on a blackboard.

Newsprint, which is an inexpensive paper, can be obtained in large sheets and fixed to a blackboard or to the walls of a building. It can be used in the same way as a blackboard but it is more versatile. Text and drawings can be prepared on several sheets, before a meeting, to avoid having to write while speaking. Paper and pens can be given to small discussion groups to note their conclusions. These conclusions can then be displayed around the meeting-place and discussed by others. Suggestions and ideas from the audience can be added to enable farmers to see their decisions taking shape. Used sheets can be kept for future reference. At a planning meeting with a group of farmers, for example, the agent can take away the sheets to guide him in preparing a written record of the decisions taken.

Posters

Posters are useful for highlighting the main theme of a talk and wall charts can be used to show complex processes.

Although they are used mainly in classroom teaching where they can be left on the wall for future reference, they can also be carried by the extension agent to help him to convey ideas to farmers.

Flip Charts

Flip charts contain a series of pictures, with or without words, fastened along one edge between two sheets of thin wood or thick cardboard. The two covers can be opened and folded back so that the flip chart stands in front of the audience. Each picture illustrates one point in the extension agent's talk and he simply turns over each one when he moves on to the next point. As well as helping the audience to understand and remember they remind the agent of the structure of his talk without the need to refer constantly to his written notes.

Many extension agents will already have access to printed posters, wall charts and flip charts, but they can also be made locally with large sheets of paper and coloured pens. When making flip charts, the following points should be noted.

- Lettering should be large.
- Diagrams should be simple.
- Information on each sheet should be limited.
- Pictures from posters and magazines can be cut out and stuck on by those who cannot draw.
- Pretesting is important for all home-made visual aids.

Flannel Graphs

A flannel Graph is made from rough textured cloth, such as flannel or a blanket, which is hung or supported almost vertically. Figures, words, and symbols cut from cardboard, which are backed with similar cloth or sandpaper, are attached to it. A cheaper backing is obtained by putting glue on the back of the cut-out and then dipping it into fine sand. The backing holds the cut-outs firmly on the cloth surface. The cut-outs are prepared beforehand and can be used repeatedly.

The flannel graph can be used very effectively to build up a story or an explanation. Unlike a wall chart, which can confuse an audience by presenting a finished diagram at the start of a talk, a flannel graph can be used to present in turn each part of the diagram until it is complete.

The cut-outs can be placed in different positions to show alternative outcomes. After showing the process of wind erosion, for example, the effect of wind-breaks can be demonstrated by placing cut-outs of trees between the wind direction and a field. Arrows representing the wind can then be deflected, and the general effect shown by putting back soil symbols on the surface of the field.

A modern alternative to flannel graphs is the magnetic board. Cut-outs are backed by a magnetic strip, that holds them firmly to a metal board. They can be used in windy conditions when flannel graph cut-outs would blow away, but they are cumbersome to transport. On the other hand, flannel graphs, which can be made in a variety of sizes and designs can be folded into an agent's bag or rolled up and tied to a bicycle.

Projected Aids

Films, colour slides, filmstrips and overhead projector transparencies are useful as teaching aids, bringing colour, variety and interest to an extension talk. However, they all require specific equipment and electricity. Extension agents are, therefore, more likely to use them in training centres and schools, although some slide projectors can be adapted to work from a 12-volt car battery. Films, filmstrips and slides are best used at night or in a room with curtains drawn or shutters closed. Daylight screens can be used for small groups.

Overhead projectors can be used in daylight, provided the sun is not shining directly on the screen or wall on which the image is projected.

Colour slides can be selected and put in a suitable sequence by the extension agent. He can produce his own slides to suit his purposes, provided he has access to a camera, film and film processing facilities. A slide set can easily be modified or updated by replacing one or more slides. If they are kept dry and free from dust and fingerprints, they will remain in good condition for many years. An agent can either provide his own spoken comments on the slides, or a commentary can be recorded on an audio-cassette. With synchronized equipment, the tape can be modified so that slides automatically change at the appropriate point.

Filmstrips

Filmstrips contain a sequence of slides in a single continuous strip of film. They are shown on a slide-projector fitted with a filmstrip carrier between the projector body and the lens. They cannot be modified easily and the sequence is fixed, but individual frames cannot fall out or be put into the projector the wrong way round. They are useful when a fixed message has to be presented many times.

Overhead projectors are usually only found in classrooms. Diagrams and texts are put on to a sheet of transparent acetate with special felt pens; the acetate is then placed on a flat glass platform through which a light shines, projecting the contents on to a vertical screen. The agent can write on the acetate while facing his audience, or he can prepare it beforehand. If he covers different parts of a sheet with paper, he can gradually reveal the sections of a diagram, thus achieving an effect similar to the flannel graph.

Using Audio-visual Aids

Audio-visual aids are only effective if they are appropriate to the situation and are used properly by the agent. Unsuitable aids or ones that are not used properly can at best distract and at worst mislead the audience. When selecting suitable audio-visual aids, the agent will be limited to what is readily available or can be made. Within that range, some aids are more suited to a particular objective than others. For example, if accurate detail is needed, a photograph, slides or a careful drawing may be more appropriate. If, on the other hand, the agent simply wants to highlight the structure of a talk or the main conclusions of a discussion, a blackboard or newsprint will be suitable. The agent should also consider where the aids will be used: indoors or outdoors, with or without electricity, at a large meeting or with a small group. All these factors will influence the choice of audio-visual aids.

Proficiency in using audio-visual aids cannot be learned from a book; it comes only with practice. The following principles may, however, be useful, whatever audio-visual aids an extension agent may use.

Select the aids most in accordance with your objective, the composition and size of the audience where the aids will be used. Use the aids to reinforce your message. They are therefor support, to complement and supplement the spoken word, and should not be expected to communicate their contents without explanation. Refer to them, explain them and ask questions about them.

Make sure that the audience will be able to see and hear clearly. Audio cassettes that cannot be heard or lettering that is too small to be seen can make the audience restless and inattentive.

Practise using the aids beforehand. Where projected aids are used, it is important to be completely accustomed to the equipment. For example, there are seven incorrect ways of loading a slide into a projector but only one correct way.

Relative Effectiveness of Methods

Two factors are considered in evaluating the relative ness of the teaching methods or channels of communication.

The success of methods in influencing people to make the desired changes desired changes. secondly the amount of the teaching effort expended on it.

The particular influence means teaching may be great because of emphasis placed on it in the extension teaching plan. Total influence of a method may be relatively small owing to little use of it in extension teaching. This explain the relatively small influence of farm visits in changing the agricultural practices.

An unit of time devoted to particular method of teaching may yield much larger returns than amount of efforts expanded on methods of teaching.

It is advisable to use a combination of teaching methods. The combination of two methods used to complement each other may be greater than the sum of the effectiveness of the same methods when employed independently. The most successful extension worker utilizes from the entire teaching efforts the best combination of the teaching methods available to him in such a manner as to ensure the possible target accomplishment. Determining the influence and cost of each method used is difficult to measure due to the informal nature of extension work and the numerous opportunities for learning available to rural people.

5

Extension Programme Planning

Extension Programmes

In previous chapters, the methods and skills that an extension agent uses in his work with farmers and their families have been examined. It has been stressed that all extension activity requires careful planning if it is to be effective. No extension activity is planned in isolation; every demonstration, public meeting or film show is part of an overall extension programme through which an extension agent and farmers work toward the agricultural development of their area. In this chapter, a number of important principles that should guide the agent in planning and evaluating extension programmes will be considered.

An extension programme is a written statement which contains the following four elements:

Objectives which the agent expects to be achieved in the area within a specified period of time. This will often be a one-year period, to enable the agent to review the programme at the start of each farming year.

Means of achieving these objectives.

Resources that are needed to fulfill the programme.

Work plan indicating the schedule of extension activities that will lead to the fulfillment of the programme objectives.

An extension programme with clearly defined objectives is helpful to local farmers, the agent himself, his senior extension officers and other rural development agencies. For the farmers, it shows both what they can expect from the extension service and how effective the agent is. For the agent, the programme provides a firm basis for planning extension activities on a monthly and weekly basis and for anticipating well in advance what resources will be needed. Senior extension officers can use programmes to assess agents' performance, to offer advice for improvement and to justify requests for additional staff, equipment and funds. Furthermore, the programme helps other agencies to coordinate their activities with what the agent is doing. However, programmes can only be used in these ways if they are written and made available to all concerned.

A written programme is also useful when staff changes bring a new agent into the area. The new agent can use the programme to carry on from where his predecessor finished, thereby ensuring continuity of activities.

All organizations involved in agricultural development have their own procedures for planning, which can vary considerably. In particular, they can differ in the extent to which plans are made at national or local level. When considering the planning of extension programmes, two different forms can be distinguished.

Planning from below. Farmers, with their extension agents, make plans for developing local agriculture on the basis of local needs and potential, and then make requests for specific assistance from national and regional authorities.

Planning from above. The agent is simply expected to implement plans made at national level. He may, for example, be given a target number of hectares to be planted with improved seeds, or a specified number of farmers' groups to set up.

Successful extension programmes should include both planning approaches. National policies and programmes provide a framework within which the agent plans his local programmes, and they establish priorities, which he must follow. If a national priority is to increase production of arable food crops rather than livestock products, the agent will give these crops a high priority in his own programme. National programmes will also make funds and inputs available for particular kinds of activity, which will influence the agent in his local planning decisions. But agricultural improvement comes from the willing action of farmers as they try to increase their own output and living standards. Local needs, therefore, provide the motivation for agricultural development, and must be taken into account in the planning of local extension programmes. Even in cases where the agent's freedom of decision is limited by national policy and directives, he must still prepare a programme that will enable him to fulfill these directives within his area.

Extension Programmes bring Together National Policies and Local Initiatives

In planning his extension programme, the agent should, therefore, balance national and local requirements. On the one hand, he should take note of national objectives but on the other hand, he should also work with local people so that the programme that emerges is theirs, and reflects their needs and what they want to see happen in the area and on their farms. This local involvement in planning is an important part of the educational process of extension. It stimulates a close analysis of farming problems and helps to build up motivation and self-confidence in using local resources to tackle them.

In some countries, agents work with formal, local-level committees when planning extension programmes. However this local involvement is achieved, the agent must take care that those who are involved can really represent the views and interests of all groups in the area. Committees often contain a high proportion of the more progressive, larger-scale farmers and are therefore inclined to promote programmes that fit the interests of these particular groups.

Process in Programme Planning

Whatever particular procedures for programme planning are laid down by the extension organization, five distinct stages can be identified.

1. *Analyze* the present situation.
2. *Set* objectives for the extension programme.
3. *Develop* the programme by identifying what needs to be done to achieve the objectives, and then prepare a work plan.
4. *Implement* the programme by putting the work plan into effect.
5. *Evaluate* the programme and its achievements as a basis for planning future programmes.

This will then lead to a review of the situation and the planning of a new programme, which should build on the achievements and learn from the failures of the previous one.

The different stages of extension programme planning are interrelated and the planning does not always proceed neatly from one stage to another. Provisional objectives, for example, may be set during the situation analysis stage, but they may later be altered as new facts are collected and a deeper analysis leads to fuller understanding of the situation. Objectives may have to be altered still further as unexpected difficulties arise while the programme is being implemented. However, it is useful for the agent to think of programme planning as involving these five activities, each of which will be considered in more detail, as each can be broken down into smaller steps.

1. Situation Analysis

Before an extension programme can be draw up, the existing situation must first be analyzed. Farming problems and their causes must be understood and the natural, human and other resources of the area identified. This stage involves three activities.

Collecting Facts

There is a good deal of information that the agent will need about the people in the area, their farming systems, natural resources and the facilities available for local development. The agent will need information in order to have a good understanding of the situation with which he is dealing, for example, on social structure and local culture, farming systems, education and literacy levels, size of farms, local channels of communication, transport facilities, local credit systems, marketing, health and nutrition levels, and crops and livestock.

These facts can be collected from a variety of sources. Reports of soil classification and land-use surveys, farm management studies, social surveys and previous programmes can provide a lot of useful background information. If the agent keeps good records of the farms in his area, he will have at his fingertips much of the information he needs. He can also obtain a lot of his information from farmers and local leaders. At public meetings, in group discussions and in contact with individual farmers, the agent should listen, ask questions and gradually build up a fuller understanding of the social, agricultural and economic features of the area.

Detailed social and economic surveys require complex questionnaires and statistical analysis, and are best left to professional researchers. But simple questionnaires can be used in this fact-finding exercise and it is helpful if the extension organization provides a standard list of questions or facts as a guide to the agent. One way in which farmers can be brought into the planning process at this early stage is for them to do some of the fact-finding themselves, using simple checklists and questionnaires, for example, to catalogue natural resources in the area.

Analyzing Facts

Facts do not speak for themselves. It is necessary to ask why things happen in the way they do. If farmers report that yields have declined in recent years, the agent must look for other information that would suggest an explanation. Is it because of low rainfall, declining soil fertility, or poor seed? The agent must also separate fact from opinion and guesswork. He may obtain conflicting information from two different sources, and must judge which is the more reliable.

Identifying Problems and Potential

It should now be possible to decide what the main problems facing farmers in the area are, and what potential there is for agricultural improvement. This is where the agent's technical knowledge becomes important. Farmers may know what their problems are, but the agent can bring his own perception of local problems based on a more scientific understanding of farming. He will be able to explain problems more fully and relate them to processes which farmers may not realize are in any way connected. Because of his training and experience, he will also have more suggestions to make about how the resources of the area could be used more productively.

Throughout the situation analysis, the agent should avoid either, relying totally on his own expertise when interpreting facts and identifying problems, or leaving it entirely up to farmers to define local needs and possibilities for change. It should be a joint effort, with agents and farmers bringing their own experience and knowledge together to reach a full understanding. If farmers are not fully involved in these activities, the agent runs the risk of misinterpreting facts, wasting time in analysis and, almost certainly, of failing to gain the full support of farmers for the programme.

A full situation analysis is not needed every year. The basic facts about the area and the people will, in most situations, not change very much from year to year. However, the agent should review basic information each year and decide which parts of it need to be updated.

2. Setting Objectives

Once the existing situation has been analyzed, decisions can be made about the changes that should be brought about through an extension programme. The key questions are how will local problems be solved and how will local potential be developed. Solutions will require clear, realistic objectives which should be set in three stages.

Finding Solutions

In looking for solutions to local problems, the agent should distinguish between technical solutions, involving improved inputs or simple changes in husbandry practice, and solutions which involve institutional changes, such as improved credit and marketing systems. Solutions involving institutional changes may require action by other agencies and at higher levels. While the agent should certainly suggest such solutions to those responsible, there may be little that can be done locally in isolation.

The sources of ideas for developing an area's potential include:

- The agent's own technical knowledge;
- Farmers and agents from other areas who have tackled similar problems successfully;
- applied research which tests new ideas under farm conditions;

- National priorities and directives;
- Projects which make funds available for particular activities.

Selecting Solutions

When selecting from among the range of solutions and possible improvements, agent and farmers should ensure that proposed solutions are:

Acceptable to farmers in the area.

Technically sound and tested by research and experience elsewhere.

Consistent with national policy, and with the local activities of other agencies.

Feasible within the time and with the resources available to farmers and the extension service.

Within the scope of the agent's ability and job description.

The agent may find that some problems will have no feasible or acceptable solution that can be implemented locally within the period of the extension programme. They may require legislation, action at other levels and by other agencies, or more research. The agent should lessen the effect of such problems where possible and act as a channel for putting forward the case for changes to those who have the power to make them.

Stating Objectives

It should now be possible to state what the objectives of the extension programme are to be. But because his time and resources may be limited, the agent must decide which objectives have a higher priority than others. In doing so, he should consider national priorities and the size and distribution of the benefits that will arise from a given input of time and resources.

Wherever possible, objectives should be expressed in terms of amounts and numbers, rather than general statements. "Establish two groups of dairy farmers who will share new equipment and market their produce jointly", and "Increase the acreage of improved rice varieties from 60 to 120 acres" are more useful objectives than "Improve dairy farming techniques" or "Increase the use of improved rice seed". They give the agent firm targets to work toward, and a standard against which the effectiveness of the programme can be judged at the end of the year.

The objectives for an annual extension programme will state what should have been achieved by the end of the programme. These statements can be broken down into intermediate steps to be taken during the year in order to achieve the programme objectives. Again, the agent will have to make choices, selecting the most appropriate steps from several possibilities.

As the agent breaks down each programme objective into specific steps, he will in effect be preparing a schedule of extension activities for the programme period. He will decide what knowledge and skills the farmers will need; what additional technical information will be required from specialists and research workers; what extension methods should be used; and what resources and support he will need from his own and other agencies.

3. Developing an Extension Programme

Problem	Local shortage of staple food.
Potential	Some local farmers have increased maize yields by 30-40 per cent by using improved seed and animal manure most farmers have plenty of manure but do not use it.

(Contd.)

Solutions	A. Increase size of small farms and intro-duce labour-saving techniques • not feasible: no access to additional land. B. Encourage larger, mechanized farms to grow more food crops • Not acceptable: poorer farm families could not buy the food. C. Enable smaller farmers to increase yields • Not feasible, using better varieties and tested husbandry improvements.
Preferred Solution C	

Objective	Raise yields by 30 per cent on 20 per cent of the farms in the area in the first year.
Intermediate objectives	50 per cent of farmers will learn of the benefits, and will acquire the skill, of using manure. 50 per cent of farmers will learn the benefits of new varieties. 20 per cent of farmers will plant improved varieties.
Plan of work	• Establish demonstration plots on ten farms. • Hold public meetings and film shows in ten villages to show the benefits of new varieties and improved husbandry. • Hold method demonstrations of manuring and correct spacing at the appropriate times. • Visit farms during planting season. • Hold result demonstrations on selected plots to encourage more farmers to try the new varieties and practices next year.
Support needed	• Subject-matter specialist to speak at public meetings, attend demonstrations and answer farmers' questions. • Adequate supplies of seeds, at the right time, at local stores. • Farm broadcasts to include relevant items at the appropriate time of year.

The simplified example on page 113 shows how the agent can develop an extension programme into a schedule of field-level activities.

When the planning is completed for other programme objectives, the agent can compile all the plans into an overall annual work plan. He may find that he cannot possibly do everything that all the individual plans require, so some of the lower priority objectives may have to be dropped, or scaled down. The annual work plan does not specify what the agent will be doing on each day during the year, but it should indicate when each extension activity will begin and end, and what resources will be needed for each.

4. Implementation

To implement the programme, the agent carries out the activities specified in the work plan. His detailed monthly and weekly plans will take account of progress and problems encountered in previous months. For example, the timing of some activities may have to be changed, or additional method demonstrations may be planned if more farmers than expected want to take part. An extension programme should be flexible enough to allow the agent to respond to circumstances in this way.

5. Evaluation

The agent will be constantly reviewing and evaluating his progress during the year. At the end of the year, a more thorough evaluation should be carried out in which the agent identifies how fully each objective has been achieved, and the reasons for any lack of progress. This evaluation, together with an up-dated situation analysis, provides the basis for planning the next year's programme.

Evaluating Extension Programmes

Evaluation is the process by which the effectiveness of extension is assessed. It is more than simply finding out what happened; it involves passing judgment on what happened. Was the outcome of the programme good enough? Was it better or worse than expected? Could more have been achieved?

Extension programmes are evaluated to (a) ascertain for the extension organization how well agents perform, so that their suitability for promotion may be assessed; (b) satisfy the government that public money spent on extension is being used effectively; and (c) permit the agent to learn from what has happened. Evaluation is a waste of time unless the results have an influence on future extension decisions.

One approach to evaluation is to ask if the programme's objectives were achieved. This is an important first step and one which is made easier if the programme had clear, precise objectives. If the answer is no, then there is no real basis on which to make improvements in future programmes. It is important, therefore, to ask why things turned out in the way they did. Only when that question is answered can the agent learn from the past. Agents should, therefore, ask questions about the following aspects of the programme.

Results. What happened as a result of the extension programme? Were they the results that were expected, and were there any unexpected results?

Inputs. Were all the planned inputs available and, if not, why?

Levels of Evaluation

There are several levels of evaluation of extension programmes. At the most general level, the effect of extension on agricultural production, family incomes and standards of living can be evaluated. An increase in family living standards is usually an important ultimate goal of rural extension and it is, therefore, important to ask whether any increase has occurred. Evaluation of this kind involves measuring production and farm income for a representative sample of farm families, and then comparing the figures with previous levels. The changes revealed by these figures are then related to the extension inputs and activities during the programme.

However, extension is not the only factor that leads to higher production and living standards; changes in prices and in the availability of inputs are two of the many additional factors that affect the level of crop and of livestock production. Separating the effects of these various factors is a complex task and best left to specialist research and evaluation staff. Nevertheless, the agent should be aware of these economic changes and regularly ask himself how much his extension activities are contributing to the economic well-being of farmers and their families. He should also observe who is benefiting from extension. Is a broad cross-section of the farming population sharing the benefits, for example, or do one or two particular groups benefit most?

An intermediate level of evaluation is provided by the extension programme itself. Two questions are important here. Did the extension activities take place in the planned sequence and at the right time? Did these activities lead to the expected results? If the answers are negative, the agent should try to understand why. Perhaps he was over-ambitious about how many extension activities he could undertake, or maybe he did not receive the support he needed from other agencies. Whatever the reason, the agent will be able to learn from the evaluation process. He should be able to make more realistic plans in the future to ensure that the necessary support and inputs are provided.

Finally, the agent can evaluate at the level of each extension activity. All extension activities, such as demonstrations, talks or meetings with a farmers' group, have a purpose. The agent should try to check, wherever possible, not only how well the activity itself was conducted but whether the purpose was achieved. This will usually involve finding out whether the extension activity led to any changes in one or more of the following:

- Awareness of a particular idea, possibility or problem;
- Motivation to act in a particular way;
- Knowledge about new farming practices;
- Skills needed to adopt a new practice;
- Behaviour by farmers and their families (such as new farming methods), or by an extension group (such as making an application for funds to carry out a group project or the preparation of a formal group constitution).

At all levels of evaluation, the agent needs to collect information to compare the situation after the activity with the situation existing before. He will already have assessed the situation before evaluation when deciding on the need for the extension activity. When planning a result demonstration, for example, he will have some idea of how many farmers in the area know about, are interested in, or have already adopted the particular practice that is to be demonstrated. However, he can obtain a more accurate assessment by asking those who attend the demonstration how much they already know and what experience they have had of the practice. By carrying out a similar assessment after the demonstration, he can collect the information he needs for evaluation.

Some effects can be assessed much sooner than others. Immediately after a public meeting, for example, the agent can talk to a few members of the audience and check how clearly they understood what he was saying. Changes in behaviour, on the other hand, will not happen at once and the agent must wait before checking these.

There are several ways of collecting information for evaluation at the village level.

Agent's reports. Whether or not a formal report of each extension activity is required from agents by their extension officers, the agent should make some notes on each activity for his own use, concentrating on his conduct of the activity and on points to note for future occasions.

Supervisors. It is not easy for an agent to assess how well he conducts an extension activity; in particular, he cannot see himself through the eyes of the farmers who attend. It is useful, therefore, to have constructive comments from a supervisor or colleague.

Discussions. Informal discussion with farmers after the extension activity will reveal their immediate reactions. It is often useful to record such discussions using a tape-recorder for later transcription and fuller analysis.

Questionnaires. Simple checklists and questionnaires can be used when the agent has the time and opportunity to carry out a more formal evaluation of extension activities. Before a result demonstration on early planting, for example, the agent could prepare a list of four or five important facts that farmers should know after they have attended. By asking a sample of farmers questions on the facts, before and after the demonstration, the agent can assess its impact on farmers' knowledge.

Observation. Where changes in farming practice are concerned, observation is an accurate source of information. The agent can see whether or not his advice is being adopted on farms in the area.

Many extension organizations have their own formal procedures for evaluation. In some, the agent prepares a detailed plan of work each month on a standard form, showing what he plans to do each day during the month and how these activities fit in with his annual extension programme. The plan of work is then used as the basis for evaluation at the end of the month. Did he do all that he planned? Did he encounter any problems that he should take into account in the future? Is he on target in terms of progress toward his annual extension programme objectives? This procedure may be combined with a monthly meeting of agents in a particular district at which progress and problems in each area are discussed.

Whatever the formal procedures in a particular organization, however, the agent should think of evaluation as an attitude of mind. He should develop a readiness to ask what happened, why it happened and how it could be done better in the future. In this way, he will continue.

Importance of Extension Programme

These programmes are very essential for planning:

1. To ensure careful consideration of what is to be done and why.
2. To furnish a guide against which new proposals are to be judged.
3. To prevent in written form a statement for public use.
4. To established objective with which progress can be measured and evaluated.
5. To have a means of choosing the important from the incidental problems and the permanent from the temporary changes.
6. To present mistaking the means for the end and to develop both felt and unfelt needs.
7. To give continuity during changes of personnel.
8. To aid in the development of leadership.

9. To avoid waste of time and money and promote general efficiency.

10. To coordinate the efforts of the different people working for rural development.

Characteristics of Programme Planning

A good programme should have the following characteristics:

1. The written programme should be suitable for the use of the staff, planning groups, and other groups and individual.

2. It should be contain primary facts that clearly reflect the situation on major subject or problem area.

3. It should be clearly state the important problems or needed identified by the staff and the people in the programming.

4. It should state both long-term and short-term objectives for each major subjects or problems that is to be focused on in programme execution over a period of time.

5. It should state the objectives of the programme clearly and meaningfully.

6. It should be specify the subject matter related to objective which is highly significant to people socially, and economically.

7. It should be include the summary of the long-term programme prepared in a form of suitable for public distribution.

8. It should be made available in a summary form to all members of the planning groups and the professional staff.

9. It should be circulated by appropriate means so that the general public can understand its nature and objective.

10. It should be used as a basis for developing an annual plan for work.

Organizations Involvement in Planning an Extension Programme

Planning is an important aspect of extension at three levels:

- The policy development level
- The programme level
- The specific activity within the programme level

Who should be Involved in the Programme?

The **change agent(s)** who must have:

- ***Credibility.*** The agent must be regarded by the community as knowledgeable about the subject and his/her motives must be trusted.
- ***Communication Skills.*** The message must be able to be conveyed simply but effectively using top-quality personal presentation skills, audio-visual material, handouts etc.
- ***Technical and Systems Skills.*** A key role of change agents is to explain the desired change in terms that can be understood by farmers and growers whose level of technical knowledge varies widely. They must also be able to assist farmers and growers to integrate the change into existing management systems.
- ***Facilitation Skills.*** They must be able to assist the audience to arrive at the solutions themselves

by asking appropriate questions and ensuring that everyone feels able to question and participate.

- Must be **enthusiastic** and able to enthuse others.

The Target Audience or Community Stakeholders

- This may be just a defined group of farmers and growers but, in the case of resource management projects, is more likely to involve wider rural communities. The attitudes, beliefs and information held by the audience must be established and a strategy devised to involve the audience in developing and implementing the solution.

- Existing community groups provide a framework from which to draw community representatives. Identifying key community groups can assist in providing an understanding of the community in which the programme is to be implemented.

- It is important that both men and women and members of different cultural groups within the affected community and from farm families are included. They each provide a different perspective and have significant influence in community responses. While men tend to be action-oriented, women often have a longer-term strategic orientation and concern for family and social aspects.

- Community leaders—their support of the programme will significantly improve the likelihood of success.

Farmers and Growers Involved in Programme

- ***Those able to demonstrate practices.*** Early adopters or operators of selected demonstration farms.

- ***Key farmers and growers.*** (Recognized by the community as leaders or particularly good farmers and growers) should be identified early to test ideas, assist in planning and assist in programme delivery.

Other advisers/service providers. Whose activities may be complementary should be included in the team if possible. It is important that there is reinforcement of the programme from as many sources in the community as possible.

The co-operation and early involvement of the media can provide positive reinforcement for an extension programme. Efforts should be made from the outset to keep local papers etc. fully informed.

Researchers' Role in the Programme

- Help to provide "solutions", and fill information gaps.
- Adapt technology to different circumstances.
- Help in problem solving.

Other Advisors/Service Providers. The community group included the local veterinarian, accountants, stock agent and bank manager to ensure that all agencies were informed about the project and could support it through their dealings with farmers and growers.

Setting the Objective of the Programme

Every extension project must have a clearly defined objective.

That Objective Must

- Be based on a demonstrable need for change.
- Be agreed upon and clearly understood by the extension agent and the target audience.
- Define the desired behaviour change in terms of a specified outcome.
- Define the target audience.

The Outcomes Defined in the Project Objective Must

- Be able to be monitored, measured and evaluated.
- Be achievable in a relatively short time or be able to be divided into a number of intermediate outcomes. Where a single end-point is achievable only in the distant future, enthusiasm will be hard to maintain.
- Be able to be measured using measures which are meaningful to the target audience. *Example: For 50% of Bay of Plenty sheep and beef farmers and growers to be aware of three monitoring techniques they can use by 30 June 1994.*

The Desired Change

- Must address some farmer perception of need, or include raising awareness of that need.
- Be technically sound—the risks of being wrong include loss of credibility.
- Have benefits for the target audience which will be demonstrated during the extension programme.
- Must be understood by the extension agent in terms of the way in which it fits into current farming practices.

- Must be understood by the extension agent in terms of all the possible outcomes for farmers and growers and their consequences.
- Must be conveyed in a small number of simple messages.

Evaluating the Programme

Evaluating extension programmes are available. The most common of these, the "Before-After Study" is a reasonably flexible and relatively inexpensive approach. The evaluation should:

- Be outlined at the start of the project although, as programmes often require modification during the time they are running, a complete evaluation process probably will not be designed at the outset.
- Be carried out by someone not connected with the programme.
- Involve one (some) of a range of questionnaire approaches from personal interview to postal survey of a sample of those affected by the programme.
- Use appropriate survey design and analysis methods. These critically affect the results of the survey. Professional advice should be sought on these issues if possible.
- It should include measurement of the following important aspects:
- Inputs—materials used
- Activities—attendance at meetings.
- People involvement—number of enquiries after the meeting.

- Reactions—reactions of participants after field-days etc.
- Practice change—adoption of the methods or techniques that were demonstrated or discussed
- End results—farmers and growers achieving the objectives

Choosing and Using the Media

The selection of media depends on:

- The usage and credibility of the medium with the target audience.
- The nature of the target audience.
- The stage in the awareness to adoption process.
- The funds available.

Several extension media were used by the facilitator of the programme:

1. ***Discussion Group.*** The community group met four times per year and effectively functioned as a discussion group whose focus was on monitoring techniques.
2. ***Newsletters.*** Describing the results of monitoring and the progress of the monitor farm were distributed to as many as possible of the Bay of Plenty farmers and growers and agribusiness people. Newsletters were used more frequently at the start of the programme when awareness was low, and less frequently towards the end.
3. ***Articles*** and some advertisements supporting the programme were published in the "New Zealand Farmer" magazine.

The remainder of this section provides detailed information on the strengths and weaknesses of a range of media-seminars, discussion groups, newsletters, field days, workshops, radio talks, and articles.

Seminars

A seminar is a meeting of 20 to 50 people at which a number of presentations on a particular subject are given. While the presentations themselves do not usually involve interaction between speakers and audience, time for discussion is usually included in the programme. The duration of a seminar ranges from one hour to one day.

Strengths

- Good medium for presentation of in-depth information
- Information can be presented from a range of perspectives, e.g. the practical implications of a soil
- conservation practice may be described by a farmer, the applicability of the practice within a district discussed by a consultant and the effectiveness of the practice as a soil conservation measure reported by a scientist.
- Provides an opportunity for the local community to have contact with a range of resource people at one time.

- Providing the programme is appropriately structured, a seminar can be an opportunity for consensus to be reached on actions to be taken.
- Sophisticated audio-visual techniques may be employed to convey information, e.g. computer-aided displays, videos etc.
- Not subject to cancellation in adverse weather.

Weaknesses

- Cannot usually involve practical demonstrations.
- Although discussion time is usually allowed, a seminar is a formal environment where audience participation is limited and less forceful people may be reluctant to air their views.
- Because a number of speakers is involved, seminars can be relatively expensive.

Can be Used

- When the audience is at the awareness and information gathering stage of an extension programme.
- To convey information in a wide range of situations except where practical examples are essential to understanding the practice.

Organizing a Seminar

Date, Time and Duration

Consider the audience and the constraints that their other activities impose (lambing, calving, harvest, milking, school holidays etc.). At a busy time it is often possible to get people to attend a two hour event during the quietest time of day although an all-day event would be impossible. Remember when dealing with farmers and growers that many partners work off-farm and that someone may need to be home to meet children returning from school.

Venue

The room must be the right size for the group and provide a comfortable environment for the participants. Check seating, lighting and heating. A light, bright room encourages open discussion.

It must be suitable for operating the audio-visual equipment required by speakers.

Use a local venue, with which participants are familiar, if it provides adequate facilities.

Programme

Structure the programme so that it leads the audience through a logical learning sequence.

Include a speaker from the local community at the outset to give credibility.

Where possible, intersperse practical with theoretical, serious with entertaining and motivating with informative presentations.

Most speakers should be limited to 20 minutes for their presentations with time for some questions before the next presentation. In-depth discussion can be held after two or three related presentations. Very few speakers are able to confine presentations to less than ten minutes.

Participants enjoy the opportunity to chat informally and time should be allowed for this during refreshment breaks.

Remember, the lecture room is not a familiar environment for most audiences.

Speakers and Chairperson

Select speakers who have relevant expertise, credibility with the target audience and are good speakers.

Provide speakers with a clear (preferably written) brief describing the purpose of the seminar, the subject to be covered by their presentations, the learning objectives to be met by the presentations and the duration of those presentations. It is useful to have a brief meeting of all speakers before the programme begins to remind them of the outcomes sought, time constraints and to encourage and motivate them. It is valuable for speakers to have undertaken a trial presentation well in advance of the seminar.

The chairperson should be independent, known to the audience personally or by reputation, able to manage the session and to keep to programme. In general the seminar organizer should not be the chairperson as it is their organizations responsibility to attend to administrative matters.

Publicity

The media selected to publicize the seminar will be chosen to reach the target audience within the constraints imposed by the project budget.

Publicity is very important; without it even the "best" seminar will fail if no one turns up!

Usually, for an event of this type, a paid advertisement would appear at least twice in relevant publications (local newspaper, farming press etc.) during the preceding two to three weeks.

Promotion of such events on rural radio broadcasts and in the farming press in smaller centers can usually be achieved at no cost, to support formal advertising.

In rural communities, local newsletters are usually widely read and delivery of fliers through the rural mail can be organized. Telephone contact with key participants and opinion leaders is of high value in ensuring a good attendance. Publicity material must answer the questions **What?,**

Why?,

Who?,

Where? and

When, and For Whom?

Audio Visual Equipment

Speakers should be encouraged to make use of audio-visual aids during presentations and to advise the seminar organizers of requirements in sufficient time to book any equipment which must be hired.

Check that all equipment is functioning in time to make repairs, if necessary, and ensure that speakers are able to use the equipment they require.

Refreshment

Refreshments served before the main part of the meeting may ease participants into the meeting.

Serving refreshments during a break in the meeting allows participants to relax and is particularly valuable where the information presented is complex or highly technical, or the seminar is longer than one and a half hours.

After a meeting, a meal can provide an opportunity for participants to discuss the programme with each other and with the resource people attending.

The selection of the appropriate time for, and type of, refreshments will depend on the time at which the seminar is held, its duration and the project budget.

Recording

Since the records of the proceedings of a seminar are often required for later evaluation or distribution to a wider audience, ensure that the responsibility for taking notes, particularly of discussion sessions, is assigned to someone. Obtain copies of speakers' notes before they leave, if possible.

Common Mistakes

- Programme is too intense, people lose concentration and there is insufficient time for discussion.
- Speakers are permitted to exceed their allotted time and the last speaker is given little time, discussion time is cut, or the seminar finishes later than advertised.
- Audio-visual equipment does not work or speakers are unfamiliar with it.
- The room is uncomfortably hot or cold and participants lose concentration.
- Chair spacing is insufficient to allow for note-taking, easy vision to the speaker and a personal space".

Discussion Groups

A discussion group is group of people who meet on a regular basis to discuss and learn about issues which they define as relevant. Such groups usually have an external facilitator. Group numbers vary from 6 to 8 members up to 18 or 20 members.

Strengths

- Provide an opportunity to look at the practical implementation of ideas.
- The group support provided can encourage the adoption of new practices.
- Sharing of ideas contributes to refinement and adoption of new technologies and practices to suit local circumstances.
- Because the members of the discussion group control its direction they tend to take more ownership of the outcomes than in situations directed by outsiders.
- Discussion groups have been proven to be effective at increasing the adoption of new practices. If they are geographically spread throughout a district they can have a major impact on the rate of change throughout the district.
- They can provide an "anchor point" for the change agent, keeping him/her appraised of the practical implications of new technologies or practices.

Weaknesses

- One or two members can dominate discussion and, therefore, the outcomes of the group.
- The change agent may be tempted to believe that the attitudes and practices of the group are representative of all members of the community.
- Discussion groups may lose their focus and drift unless they are continually rejuvenated by the

inclusion of new members, by addressing new issues and new approaches to issues.

Can be Used

- At all stages of the adoption process, but because of their practical focus, are particularly relevant to the decision and implementation phase.
- Particularly relevant for introducing a new practice into a district.

Organizing a Discussion Group

Selection of Group Members

The change agent should liaise with two or three key participants and, with them, prepares a list of prospective group members. They are telephoned and invited to attend an initial meeting.

Date, Time and Duration

Discussion groups typically meet monthly, at least at the outset, at a time decided by members of the group. The duration of each meeting will depend on the issues to be addressed, but with farming discussion groups is usually half a day.

Venue

Discussion group meetings are usually held on the properties of each of the group members in turn. There must be some indoor facility in which members can hold the discussion in moderate comfort.

Programme

The topic for each meeting is determined by the group. The programme is then arranged by the facilitator and the chairperson.

At each meeting there is usually a farm walk or a practical demonstration followed by a presentation on a topic of interest by the facilitator or an invited guest speaker and a group discussion on that topic and others of interest. It is common for the group to make recommendations about aspects of the management of the property on which it is meeting.

Groups may also visit other properties, or places of interest, to pursue specific issues.

Group Structure

The discussion group is usually initiated by the change agent who acts as the facilitator. At the first meeting the group elects a chairperson, establishes its ground rules (confidentiality, extent to which financial information will be shared etc.), and decides on the issues to addressed during the next period. The practical details of meeting organization etc. are attended to by the facilitator.

Visitors to established discussion groups, hoping to use those groups as part of an extension programme rather than to establish new groups, must be aware of each group's structure and the manner in which it operates.

Group Facilitation

The facilitation of groups is a learned skill on which there are a range of references, courses etc. available. Any change agent proposing to use discussion groups as a medium should ensure that they undertake adequate training, as the success of the group may depend on this to a large extent.

Publicity

It is the facilitator's responsibility to distribute notices of meeting to members. Most discussion groups also have a telephone "tree" system for communication when necessary.

Recording

Notes on the property to be visited, and on any special topics to be discussed, may be prepared and distributed to members by the facilitator.

Common Mistakes

- The facilitator provides technical solutions rather than helping the group to "learn" and find its own solutions.
- If the group is not actively involved in tackling issues, members will perceive a lack of progress and cease to attend.
- If the seating arrangement has too much distance between group members (> 7 m across group), or the room is "uncomfortable" for some other reason, discussion will not flow.

Field Days

Field days are events, organized on site, to demonstrate practices or technologies and to present information. They usually cater for audiences of between 30 and 200. A field day combines a range of practical demonstrations, verbal presentations and opportunities for discussions with resource people. Field days addressing specific issues, as part of an extension programme, are more structured than large, often annual events, which include many trade exhibits and attract very large audiences.

Strengths

- "Seeing is believing". Seeing the practice in operation and being able to examine in detail how it operates is vital to the practice of adoption.

- Plenty of opportunity to interact with the speakers at group and individual levels and to have questions answered.

- Participants are in a familiar environment, the atmosphere is relaxed and informal. There is a significant social aspect to attending field days.

- A message can be conveyed to large groups at one time while still retaining a degree of personal interaction. (Most people will need additional contact, one-to-one or small group, to support their adoption decision).

- Provides an opportunity to learn informally by observation or discussion about other practices which are not the main topic of the day (e.g. a new fencing method).

Weaknesses

- Can be disrupted by adverse weather.

- Relatively expensive.

Can be Used

- At the information gathering phase before the adoption decision is made, when there is something to demonstrate physically to the audience.

Organizing A Field Day

Date, time and duration

Consider the audience and the constraints that their other activities impose (lambing, calving, harvest, milking, school holidays etc.). The date may be determined by the practice being demonstrated or the adoption time-frame hoped for. Some practices can only be implemented, and therefore demonstrated, at particular times. Where it is hoped that participants will adopt the recommended practice during the coming year it must be demonstrated in time for them to complete the adoption decision and include it in their management systems.

Venue

If possible, select the property of someone well-known and respected since this attracts participants. The property owner is usually a key speaker at a field day so her/his credibility will be a key determinant of success.

The field day must be well sign-posted from main roads.

Have a contingency plan for bad weather (move into sheds etc., erect marquees, use nearby local hall, postponement procedure).

Programme

Identify suitable demonstration areas and prepare them well in advance.

Schedule the property owner to speak at the start of the programme to provide a description of the property in order to set the context.

If the audience is expected to be fewer than 60 people, the group can proceed together to each of a series of three to five stopping points. Larger groups should be split and several displays should be running concurrently and repeated several times. At very large field days participants can be given a choice of which speakers or demonstrations are most relevant to them.

Each presentation should be less than 15 minutes and allow time for demonstrations and discussion.

Allow time for travel between displays. If necessary arrange transport between distant displays (four-wheeled-drive vehicles, tractors with trailers etc.).

Participants enjoy the opportunity to chat informally and time should be allowed for this during refreshment breaks.

Speakers

Select speakers who have relevant expertise, credibility with the target audience and are good speakers.

Provide speakers with a clear (preferably written) brief describing the purpose of the field day, the subject to be covered by their presentations, a learning objective to be met by the presentation and the duration of those presentations. It is useful to have a brief meeting of all speakers before the programme begins to remind them of the outcomes sought, time constraints and to encourage and motivate them. It is valuable for speakers to have undertaken a trial presentation well in advance of the field day.

The change agent is usually responsible for controlling the progress of the field day.

A special guest may be invited to welcome participants and provide a summary at the end of the day.

Publicity

The media selected to publicize the field day will be chosen to reach the target audience within the constraints imposed by the project budget.

Usually for an event of this type a paid advertisement would appear at least twice in relevant publications (local newspaper, farming press etc.) during the preceding two to three weeks.

Promotion of such events on rural radio broadcasts, and in the farming press in smaller centers, can usually be achieved at no cost to support formal advertising.

In rural communities, local newsletters are usually widely read and also delivery of fliers through the rural mail can be organized.

Telephone contact with key participants and opinion leaders is of value in ensuring a good attendance.

Publicity material must answer the questions

What?,

Why?,

Who?,

Where?,

When? and

For Whom?.

Audio Visual Equipment

There must be an adequate public address system and organizers must insist that speakers use this even if they are initially reluctant.

Set up display boards in advance and ensure that they are well secured against wind.

Printing on display boards should be large and bold. Displays should be simple, bright and attractive. They should not be mainly text.

Speakers should be encouraged to make use of audio-visual aids during presentations and to advise the field day organizers of requirements in sufficient time to book any equipment which must be hired.

Check that all equipment is functioning in time to make repairs if necessary and ensure that speakers are able to use the equipment they require.

Audience Comfort

Ensure the audience is comfortable while listening to presentations (hay bales to sit on, not looking into sun, shelter from wind or sun).

Refreshment

Serving refreshments during a break in the field day allows participants to relax and is particularly valuable where the information presented is complex or highly technical, or the seminar is longer than one and a half hours.

The selection of the appropriate time for, and type of, refreshments will depend on the time at which the field day is held, its duration and the project budget.

Common Mistakes

- Visual aids are not readable from the distance most people are at and flap in the wind.
- Speakers elect to not use the public address system and are not audible.
- Field days are turned into outdoor seminars. There is too little time spent "seeing and doing" relative to the time spent "hearing".
- Speakers are permitted to exceed their allotted time and the last speaker is given little time, discussion time is cut or the field day finishes later than advertised.
- Audio-visual equipment does not work or speakers are unfamiliar with it.

Workshops

A workshop, in the context of a rural community extension programme, is a meeting of 6 to 30 people who come together to discuss a common problem and to discuss solutions or programmes to be implemented. Most of the time in a workshop is spent in interactive group activity. It is usually led by an experienced facilitator. The duration of a workshop in this context ranges from half to one day or longer.

Strengths

- Provides a forum for community groups to participate in problem definition, in identifying solutions and developing implementation strategies.
- Experts can be drawn into the workshop forum to provide information but do not assume control of the proceedings. Local ownership is retained.
- Participants can develop a rapport with each other and work as a team.

Weaknesses

- Participants become involved by invitation, which may offend members of the community who are not invited.
- The process of invitation may introduce bias to the outcomes of the workshop.

Can be Used

- Problem definition—to clarify and agree current situation and whether action is required.
- Programme design—to develop a plan of action which will address a stated problem.
- Programme evaluation—to obtain feedback on progress to date, strengths and weaknesses, and programme direction.

Organizing a Workshop

Facilitator

The success of the workshop will be largely dependent on the experience and skills of the facilitator. The facilitator must be capable of:

- Stimulating and motivating participants.
- Dealing with group tensions.
- Leading the group in a range of participation techniques.
- Challenging the group if necessary.
- Leading the group through a "proven" process to reach its desired outcomes.

Date, Time and Duration

To be decided after close liaison with invited group members and consideration of the issues to be discussed. A pre-workshop planning session with some members of the group is of value in planning the workshop.

Venue

The room must be the right size for the group and provide a comfortable environment for the participants. Check seating, lighting and heating. A light, bright room encourages open discussion. There must be a number of smaller rooms available for small sub-group discussions.

It must be suitable for operating any audio-visual equipment required.

Use a local venue, with which participants are familiar, if it provides adequate facilities.

Programme

Structure the programme to lead participants to reach the desired end-point of the workshop. The workshop should start with introductions of all those present, followed by an introduction to the workshop which should cover the purpose, the desired outcomes and the programme. At this point the "ground rules" for the workshop (e.g. smoking, confidentiality of information, etc.) and the process to be followed should be agreed by the group.

The programme could include:

- Information sessions, which may include presentations from experts;
- Reflections—to learn of previous solutions or responses and of the background to the issue;
- Visioning—see a solution in the future then decide how to get there;
- Brainstorming sessions in which new ideas or options are developed;
- Decision making sessions in which priorities are set, and responsible for actions allocated, and planning sessions in which action plans are developed;

Any workshop programme must be flexible to allow the group to meet its objectives.

Participants

- The facilitator will control the workshop process (not the outcomes).
- Participants should include a mixture of people who hold a range of views on the topic under consideration and include representatives of all stakeholders in the issue.

Publicity

Usually participants are individually invited by telephone and/or mail. It may be appropriate to distribute background material before the workshop.

Audio Visual Equipment

- The usual equipment will be required for any presentations.
- Whiteboards, particularly electronic, photocopying whiteboards, are very useful for recording key points of discussion. At least one whiteboard and flip-chart is required for each sub-group.

Refreshment

Start with refreshments to help participants to get to know each other. Other refreshment breaks should be scheduled at appropriate times.

Recording

Since the records of proceedings of a workshop are often required for later evaluation or distribution to a wider audience, ensure that the responsibility of taking notes, particularly of discussion sessions, is assigned to someone. Obtain copies of any outside speakers' notes before they leave, if possible.

Common Mistake

- Under estimation of the ability of community members to contribute to problem solving and programme development in a workshop framework.
- Not inviting representatives of all stakeholders.
- Trying to progress an issue too far in one meeting. Participants need time between meetings to formulate ideas and get "comfortable" with new concepts.
- Facilitator dominates the meeting and participants become frustrated and may not be committed to the meeting outcomes.

Radio Talks

There are a number of formats in which messages may be disseminated by radio. They include radio talks which are short (two to three minute) and deal with specific subjects, news items and interviews. Radio talks, which are dealt with in this section, are the most controllable format for the change agents.

Interviews and news material are usually sought by the broadcaster although he/she may be informed about the project by the change agent. Although change agents have less control over what is finally broadcast.

Strengths

- Has a large potential audience.
- Rural bulletins are usually well-listened to by the rural community.
- Radio is an entertaining medium, which helps people absorb the message.

Weaknesses

- Does not provide the opportunity for "seeing" or "doing" and is, therefore, not appropriate for teaching new skills.

- Radio messages are immediate so the audience has no opportunity to revisit and reconsider the message if it has not remembered it accurately.
- As with all mass media, the presenter doesn't get feedback through interaction with the audience.
- Can be used.
- Particularly to create awareness of a practice.
- To provide up-dated information on progress or new developments.
- To disseminate specific technical information provided it can be conveyed simply and clearly.

Organizing a Radio Talk

Choosing a subject

- Consider which questions the community is asking about the issue, new ideas and practices and threats which people need to know about.
- Choose one aspect of the topic. It should be topical, original, applicable, rewarding or threatening, informative, newsworthy (conflict, progress, unusualness, human interest).

Planning and Constructing an Outline

- Develop a specific aim for the talk, based on the required response from the audience.
- Subject sentence—a general statement summarizing the whole subject.
- A series of main supporting statements which explain, support, illustrate, qualify or expand each idea in the subject sentence.

- Some supporting statements amplifying the main supporting statements in the same way.
- A short snappy conclusion which preferably calls for some action.
- Finally write down an opening statement which is an "ear catcher".
- Address the radio audience as if you are talking to an individual member of the community. In developing the script, say it aloud one or two sentences at a time or use a Dictaphone. To make the talk interesting, make it personal, deliver it in the active, present tense and limit it to the main points of the subject. Use local references and personal experiences as illustrations and repeat main points. Interpret research data as simply as you can and avoid figures where possible, presenting the essential ones as comparisons.

Delivery of the Script

The talk should be delivered with warmth and enthusiasm. Speak clearly, vary the speed of delivery, use plenty of pauses and vary your inflection. Practice the talk thoroughly. You should take the opportunity for a trial presentation in the studio and seek feedback from the broadcaster.

Overact while talking to the radio. Normal talking sounds flat. Using body language helps to convey an active message.

Common Mistakes

- Talk too long, too much detailed information included.
- Monotonous-lack of variation in voice, information not concise and "hard-hitting".

Making a Presentation

There are many different situations in which you will be called upon to make a presentation. These range from conferences, to discussion groups, to radio talks.

The keys to making a successful presentation are the same, whatever the forum:

Planning, Preparation, Practice and Poise or Confidence

Planning

Get clear instructions from the chairman or facilitator. These should tell you:

- Who is in the audience?
- The audience's existing knowledge of the topic.
- Nature of the venue.
- The amount of time you have been allocated.
- Your topic and what others will be speaking on.
- The learning objective for the session.

You should then restate the learning objective to ensure it says specifically what change is desired in the audience, "How do you want your audience to change as a result of your talk?" This should be a single outcome, e.g., "For audience to know importance of flushing for high lambing per centage."

Preparation

Then prepare a structure for your talk. This should have:

- Introduction—tell them what you are going to tell them;
- Body—tell them the main points and supporting statements;

- Conclusion—tell them what you have told them and call to action.

Your audience will probably only remember three things from your presentation so keep it to 5 or 6 main points with a simple "take home" message. Include examples and personal experiences that make the talk topical, applicable, rewarding or threatening, informative and newsworthy.

Having written your presentation, talk it through and edit it rigorously. Remember, written material sounds forced when spoken: Most people speak less formally than they write.

Visual Aids

Using visual aids in a presentation significantly increases your success in communicating by appealing to the sight sense. This reinforces your audiences learning through listening to your talk.

Visual aids should:

- Reinforce the topic of the presentation (not distract);
- Be "visual" i.e. use images and pictures not just words;
- Be simple, particularly graphs;
- Be big enough to be easily seen;
- When words are used there should not be more than 6 lines per overhead or 6 words per line;
- Be real examples e.g. a block of cheese or piece of soil can appeal to the sense of touch and smell as well to the sight sense.

If you have a good visual aid then let it talk for you, do not labor the points by restating them verbally.

Three golden rules, visual aids must:

- Reinforce your talk;
- Be simple;
- Be seen by all.

Equipment

When using a whiteboard, use bold colours (black or blue). Avoid red and green as these are hard to see, particularly for colour-blind people.

Make sure that the organizer will have all the equipment you need on hand. You should get there early and test it personally to ensure you know where the controls are and that it is operating properly.

Practice

Having prepared your presentation and visual aids, you should practice it several times until you are nearly ad lib and your notes are needed only as prompts. Time your practice and ensure it is well within your time allocation. Normally you will speak slower in front of your audience and you will have interruptions.

If it is too long, cut out a whole section. If possible rehearse in front of a group of colleagues. Their feedback will enhance your presentation on the day. Finally, identify a section you can leave out if your allocated time is reduced on the day.

Poise in Your Presentation

On the day present your talk with confidence. While you may feel nervous your audience cannot detect it.

Some Tips

- Stand in a relaxed open fashion and talk in a louder than normal volume;

- Make eye contact with all parts of the audience at various stages;
- Control any distracting behaviour—clicking biros, excessive raising of hands etc. If necessary put one hand behind your back;
- Make sure you are not obscuring the visual aid by standing in the wrong position;
- Vary the speed and volume of your voice;
- If a microphone is provided, use it;
- Do not worry about pauses, what seems like an "eternity" to you is only a few seconds to the audience. Pauses can be used to add impact to your presentation;
- Keep time yourself or ask the chairman to tell you when you have 2-5 minutes left.

The total impact of a presentation and the audience's learning is determined by a wide range of factors. Body language, tone and quality of voice, the content and the appeal to a range of senses-visual, auditory, touch, etc.

Newsletters

A newsletter can be produced regularly, or on an ad-hoc basis, to disseminate information to all members of a target audience. It is usually between one and three pages in length and can address one specific issue in detail or a number of issues briefly.

Strengths

- The author controls the information distributed to the target audience (this may not be the case in other print media).

- Newsletters can be prepared and delivered rapidly and are, therefore, responsive to changing situations.
- A high quality document can be produced at little cost, using modern desk-top publishing methods.
- A means of providing information to a large target audience at one time.

Weaknesses

- A vast quantity of printed material including "junk mail" is received by farmers and growers and householders. Distributors of newsletters risk having them left unread for some time.
- If the change agent is not skilled at writing, the process of producing a newsletter can be time-consuming, and the end-product may not compete successfully with other material for the reader's attention.

Can be Used

- Throughout an extension programme, to inform a wider audience about developments on the issue, in the region or within the group with which the change agent is working intensively.
- To provide regular updates to members of the target audience when there is not access to a regular column in local newspapers. If such access is available, it is generally more cost effective to use it than to produce regular newsletters.
- To disseminate information required by the audience to react to a specific event (e.g. snow storm).

Organizing A Newsletter

Content

Draft the material to be included then edit it to a clear concise form. Newsletter articles should be written in an informal manner—as much like direct speech as possible.

Material may be presented in question and answer format, as bullet points on a topic or as short articles. Important points should be made at the start of each article since many readers will read only the opening paragraphs.

The material included may be written by the change agent or reprinted from other publications. If material is copied directly, the author's permission or in the case of copyrighted material, permission from the owner of the copyright must be obtained. While reports on, or summaries of, articles or presentations do not require the original author's permission, acknowledgement should be given.

Remember "Less is More"

Keep it short and to the point with not too much information.

Layout

Newsletters which are part of a series should have a distinctive title.

The headlines must be worded to convey the main message of the article, as many members of the target audience will read only the headlines of the newsletter.

Present material so that the most important material has the highest impact (prominent position on first page, bold type-face, use of text boxes, shading etc.).

"A picture is worth a thousand words". Use plenty of visual material in different forms (cartoons, graphs, diagrams etc.) to make points. There is no need to restate points made visually, in the text.

Ensure that each page has an uncluttered appearance.

Use the same colored paper each time so that readers will more readily identify the newsletter.

The newsletter should be set out in a manner which facilitates folding to the least costly size for distribution. (Check requirements with NZ Post)

Distribution

The method of distribution will depend on the target audience. If only some members of a rural community are to receive the newsletter it must be addressed and posted normally. If all householders in an area are to receive copies, New Zealand Post will deliver copies with the rural mail and addresses will not be required.

Common Mistakes

- Material which is too long or too complex results in a low reading rate.
- Repeating in the text messages which are clearly expressed by the illustrations.

Articles

Articles can be published in a range of publications from local newspapers to national magazines. The format can vary from relatively short articles with a simple message to longer articles which include detailed analyses of a subject. Diagrams and tables can be included if required. The change agent may write his/her own article, or be interviewed by a reporter who will then produce the article.

Strengths

- Articles have a large potential audience whose size depends on the publication's circulation.

- Can be targeted to specific geographic regions (local newspapers) or grower groups (agricultural/horticultural sector publications).
- Readers can refer back to the article to clarify issues and refresh memories.
- A local change agent may be able to acquire a regular, fortnightly or monthly, column in a local newspaper.

Weaknesses

- Newspapers are frequently not well read because of competition from more "entertaining" media such as television or radio.

Can be Used

- To create awareness of a practice.
- To give detailed "how to" information about a practice.
- To publicize the results of a programme or to advertise a field day or seminar.
- To present profiles of members of the local community who have implemented a practice and report the benefits they have perceived from implementation.

Organizing an Article

Choosing a Subject

- Consider which questions the community is asking about the issue, new ideas and practices and threats which people need to know about.
- Choose one aspect of the topic. It should be topical, original, applicable, rewarding or threatening,

informative, newsworthy (conflict, progress, unusualness, human interest).

- Conducting the interview before drafting the article. The draft will usually be checked with the interviewee before publication and the change agent should always request that this is done.

Common Mistakes

- Sentences that are unclear, too long and reflect "woolly thinking".
- Article is not edited sufficiently to make it easy to read and interesting. Articles are frequently too long.
- The title and first paragraph do not convey the main ideas. Remember, many readers "skim read" a newspaper. If the title is interesting they may read the first paragraph. If the article has not captured their attention and given them the main message by that time they are unlikely to continue reading.
- Article is too complicated with long words and sentences. Remember your article should be easy to read by your audiences and many have a relatively low reading age.

The Content of an Extension Programme

- Should be as simple as possible—ideally do not attempt to convey more than three messages.
- Must be relevant to the farmer participants—change agents must ensure that they become familiar, through discussion not assumption, with what is relevant to the farmer groups with whom they are to work. If possible "work up" the programme with key stakeholders to get ownership of the problem and solution.

- The issue(s) should be addressed in terms of the interests/concerns of all participants—male/female, farmers and growers/farm families, differing cultural backgrounds etc.

- The knowledge and information held by farmers and growers must be integrated into the programme.

- Must demonstrate the benefits and costs to the participants.

- The messages should, where possible, be positive (focus on good practices) rather than negative (focus on avoiding poor practices).

- The practical implications of the behaviour change need to be discussed fully.

- The amount of material presented at any time must not exceed the group's saturation point. The greater the change being advocated and the more complicated the material, the sooner saturation point is reached.

- The programme should be fun to be involved in—interesting and varied material/activities, social interaction etc. If the programme is boring it will be impossible to make people enthusiastic.

- Use "stepwise" progress towards the end-points with clear milestones on the way.

The content of the programme was directed by the members of the community group and conducted in a real farming environment. Consequently, by definition it was relevant, addressed the concerns of participants and integrated the knowledge and information held by farmers and growers. Demonstration of the benefits to the community group farmers and growers, and subsequently publicizing them to the wider farming community, was a primary objective and discussion of the practical implications an integral part of the programme. The community group dictated the pace of the programme.

The Importance of the Environment

- Farmers and growers discuss things more freely in environments where they are comfortable. Meetings etc. should be carried out on neutral ground—preferably familiar to the participants. For many farmers and growers a formal learning environment is not "natural" and less formal surroundings, particularly "on-farm" will be more comfortable. Meetings should not be held on the premises of the organization promoting the behavior change.

- Discussion also flows more freely when participants are comfortable and/or familiar with each other. The use of outside, independent facilitators often makes people feel more comfortable, while it would be difficult for a facilitator involved in regulation enforcement to give the appearance of an independent extension agent. It is important that the programme is not used to push any political agenda since this will "turn-off" participants who do not support that agenda.

- The programme must move at the pace desired by the target audience—the programme will not be successful if it is carried out too rapidly for the participants, making them feel uncomfortable. It is most important that farmers and growers are not made to feel patronized by people who have a more academic approach.

- Socialising before a meeting, time for a chat, something to eat and drink, may ease participants into the main part of the meeting. Socialising after a meeting may allow participants to reinforce or confirm learning during the meeting.

Support for the Programme

The enthusiasm of change agents is a key factor in programme success and will be maintained through the demanding task of running the programme only if adequate support is provided.

- Managerial support within the extension agency including positive feedback.
- Political support from the agency desiring change e.g. regional or district council.
- A high level of administrative support is required, particularly for programmes of longer duration.
- Implementing a longer term extension programme requires both initiating extension agents and others prepared to carry the programme on.

People Involvement in Programme Planning

Successful extension programmes should include both planning approaches. National policies and programmes provide a framework within which the agent plans his local programmes, and they establish priorities, which he must follow. If a national priority is to increase production of arable food crops rather than livestock products, the agent will give these crops a high priority in his own programme. National programmes will also make funds and inputs available for particular kinds of activity, which will influence the agent in his local planning decisions. But agricultural improvement comes from the willing action of farmers as they try to increase their own output and living standards. Local needs, therefore, provide the motivation for agricultural development, and must be taken into account in the planning of local extension programmes. Even in cases where the agent's freedom of decision is limited by national policy and directives, he must still prepare a programme that will enable him to fulfill these directives within his area.

Extension Programmes bring Together National Policies and Local Initiatives

In planning his extension programme, the agent should, therefore, balance national and local requirements. On the one hand, he should take note of national objectives but on the other hand, he should also work with local people so that the programme that emerges is theirs, and reflects their needs and what they want to see happen in the area and on their farms. This local involvement in planning is an important part of the educational process of extension. It stimulates a close analysis of farming problems and helps to build up motivation and self-confidence in using local resources to tackle them.

In some countries, agents work with formal, local-level committees when planning extension programmes. However this local involvement is achieved, the agent must take care that those who are involved can really represent the views and interests of all groups in the area. Committees often contain a high proportion of the more progressive, larger-scale farmers and are therefore inclined to promote programmes that fit the interests of these particular groups.

Government Involvement in Programme Planning

The government has initiated, sustained, and refined many programmes since independence to help the poor attain self-sufficiency in food production. Probably the most important initiative has been the supply of basic commodities, particularly food at controlled prices, available throughout the country. The poor spend about 80 per cent of their income on food while the rest of the population spends more than 60 per cent. The price of food is a major determinant of wage scales. Often when food prices rise sharply, rioting and looting follow. Until the late 1970s, the government frequently had difficulty obtaining adequate grain supplies in years of poor harvests. During those times states with surpluses of grain were cordoned off to force partial sales to public agencies and to keep private traders from shipping grain to deficit areas to secure very high prices; state governments in surplus grain areas were often less than cooperative. After the late 1970s, the central government, by holding reserve stocks and importing grain adequately and early, maintained sufficient supplies to meet the increased demand during drought years. It also provided more remunerative prices to farmers.

In rural areas, the government has undertaken programmes to mitigate the worst effects of adverse monsoon rainfall which affects not only farmers but village artisans and traders when the price of grain rises. The government has supplied water by financing well digging and, since the early 1980s, by power-assisted well drilling, rescinded land taxes for drought areas; tried to maintain stable food prices; and provided food through a food-for-work programmes is often a secondary consideration, but useful projects sometimes result. Employment is offered at a low daily wage, usually paid in grain, the rationale being that only the truly needy will take jobs at such low pay.

In the 1980s and early 1990s, Indian government programmes attempted to provide basic needs at stable, low prices to increase income through pricing and regulations, such as supplying water from irrigation works, fertilizer, and other inputs, to foster location of industry in backward areas; to increase access to basic social services, such as education, health, and potable water supply, and to help needy groups and deprived areas. The total money spent on such programmes for the poor was not discernible from the budget data, but probably exceeded 10 per cent of planned budget outlays.

India has had a number of antipoverty programmes since the early 1960s. These include among others, the National Rural Employment Programme and the Rural Landless Employment Guarantee Programme. The National Rural Employment Programme evolved in FY 1980 from the earlier Food and Work Programme to use unemployed and underemployed workers to build productive community assets. The Rural Landless Employment Guarantee Programme was instituted in FY 1983 to address the plight of the hard-core rural poor by expanding employment opportunities and building the rural infrastructure as a means of encouraging rapid economic growth. There were many problems with the implementation of these and other schemes, but observers credit them with helping reduce poverty. To improve the effectiveness of the National Rural Employment Programme, in 1989 it was combined with the Rural Landless Employment Guarantee Programme and renamed Jawahar Rozgar Yojana, or Jawahar Employment Plan (see Development Programmes, Ch. 7).

State governments are important participants in antipoverty programmes. The constitution assigns responsibility to the states in a number of matters, including ownership, redistribution, improvement, and taxation of land (see The Constitutional Framework, Ch. 8). State governments implement most central government programmes concerned with land reform and the situation of small landless farmers. The central government tries to establish programmes and norms among the states and union territories, but implementation has often remained at the lower bureaucratic levels. In some matters concerning subsoil rights and irrigation projects, the central government exerts political and financial leverage to obtain its objectives, but the states sometimes modify or retard the impact of central government policies and programmes.

Development Planning

Planning in India dates back to the 1930s. Even before independence, the colonial government had established a planning board that lasted from 1944 to 1946. Private industrialists and economists published three development plans in 1944. India's leaders adopted the principle of formal economic planning soon after independence as an effective way to intervene in the economy to foster growth and social justice.

The Planning Commission was established in 1950. Responsible only to the prime minister, the commission is independent of the cabinet. The prime minister is chairperson of the commission, and the minister of state with independent charge for planning and programme implementation serves as deputy chairperson. A staff drafts national plans under the guidance of the commission; draft plans are presented for approval to the National Development Council, which consists of the Planning Commission and the chief ministers of the states. The council can make changes in the draft plan. After council approval, the draft is presented to the cabinet and subsequently to Parliament, whose approval makes the plan an operating document for central and state governments (see The Legislature; Local Government, Ch. 8).

The First Five-Year Plan (FY 1951-1955) attempte to stimulate balanced economic development while correcting imbalances caused by World War II and partition. Agriculture, including projects that combined irrigation and power generation, received priority. By contrast, the Second Five-Year Plan (FY 1956-1960) emphasized industrialization, particularly basic, heavy industries in the public sector, and improvement of the economic infrastructure. The plan also stressed social goals, such as more equal distribution of income and extension of the benefits of economic development to the large number of disadvantaged people. The Third Five-Year

Plant (FY 1960-1965) aimed at a substantial rise in national and per capita income while expanding the industrial base and rectifying the neglect of agriculture in the previous plan. The third plan called for national income to grow at a rate of more than 5 per cent a year; self-sufficiency in foodgrains was anticipated in the mid-1960s.

Economic difficulties disrupted the planning process in the mid-1960s. In 1962, when a brief war was fought with china on the Himalayan frontier, agricultural output was stagnating, industrial production was considerably below expectations and the economy was growing at about half of the planned rate (see Nehrus Legacy, Ch. 1). Defense expenditures increased sharply, and the increased foreign air needed to maintain development expenditures eventually provided 28 per cent of public development spending. Midway through the third plan, it was clear that its goals could not be achieved. Food prices rose in 1963, causing rioting and looting of grain warehouses in 1964. War with Pakistan in 1965 sharply reduced the foreign aid available. Successive severe droughts in 1965 and 1966 further disrupted the economy and planning. Three annual plans guided development between FY 1966 and FY 1968 while plan policies and strategies were re-evaluated. Immediate attention centered on increasing agricultural growth, stimulating exports, and searching for efficient uses of industrial assets. Agriculture was to be expanded, largely through the supply of inputs to take advantage of new high-yield seeds becoming available for foodgrains. The rupee was substantially devalued in 1966, and export incentives were adjusted to promote exports. Controls affecting industry were simplified, and greater reliance was placed on the price mechanism to achieve industrial efficiency.

The Fourth Five-Year Plan (FY 1969-1973) called for a 24 per cent increase over the third plan in real terms of public development expenditures. The public sector accounted for

60 per cent of plan expenditures, and foreign aid contributed 13 per cent of plan financing. Agriculture, including irrigation, received 23 per cent of public outlays: the rest was mostly spent on electric power industry, and transportation. Although the plan projected national income growth at 5.7 per cent a year, the realized rate was only 3.3 per cent.

The Fifth Five-Year Plan (FY 1974-1978) was drafted in late 1973 when crude oil prices were rising rapidly; the rising prices quickly forced a series of revisions. The plan was subsequently approved in late 1976 but was terminated at the end of FY 1977, because a new government wanted different priorities and programmes. The fifth plan was in effect only one year, although it provided some guidance to investments throughout the five-year period. The economy operated under annual plans in FY 1978 and FY 1979.

The Sixth Five-Year Plan (FY 1980-1984) was intended to be flexible and was based on the principle of annual "rolling" plans. It called for development expenditures of nearly Rs 1.9 trillion (in FY 1979 prices), of which 90 per cent would be financed from domestic sources, 57 per cent of which would come from the public sector. Public sector development spending would be concentrated in energy (29 per cent); agriculture and irrigation (24 per cent); industry including mining (16 per cent); transportation (16 per cent); and social services (14 per cent). In practice, slightly more was spent on social services at the expense of transportation and energy. The plan called for GDP growth to increase by 5.1 per cent a year, a target that was surpassed by 0.3 per cent. A major objective of the plan was to increase employment, especially in rural areas, in order to reduce the level of poverty. Poor people were given cows, bullock carts, and handlooms; however, subsequent studies indicated that the income of only about 10 per cent of the poor rose above the poverty level.

The Seventh Five-Year Plan (FY 1985-1989) envisioned a greater emphasis on the allocation of resources to energy and social spending at the expense of industry and agriculture. In practice, the main increase was in transportation and communications, which took up 17 per cent of public sector expenditure during this period. Total spending was targeted at nearly Rs 3.9 trillion, of which 94 per cent would be financed from domestic resources, including 48 per cent from the public sector. The planners assumed that public savings would increase and help finance government spending. In practice that increase did not occur; instead, the government relied on foreign borrowing for a greater share of resources than expected.

The schedule for the Eight Five-Year Plan (FY 1962-1996) was affected by changes of government and by growing uncertainty over what role planning could usefully perform in a more liberal economy. Two annual plans were in effect in FY 1990 and FY1991. The eighth plan was finally launched in April 1992 and emphasized market-based policy reform rather than quantitative targets. Total spending was planned at Rs 8.7 trillion, of which 94 per cent would be financed from domestic resources, 45 per cent of which would come from the public sector. The eighth plan included three general goals. First, it sought to cut back the public sector by selling off failing and inessential industries while encouraging private investment in such sectors as power, steel and transport. Second it proposed that agriculture and rural development have priority. Third, it sought to renew the assault on illiteracy and improve other aspects of social infrastructure, such as the provision of fresh drinking water. Government documents issued to 1992 indicated that GDP growth was expected to increase form around 5 per cent a year during the seventh plan to 5.6 per cent a year during the eighth plan. However, in 1994 economists expected annual growth to be around 4 per cent during the period of the eighth plan.

Four decades of planning show that India's economy, a mix of public and private enterprise, is too large and diverse to be wholly predictable or responsive to directions of the planning authorities. Actual results usually differ in important respects from plan targets. Major shortcomings include insufficient improvement in income distribution and alleviation of poverty, delayed completions and cost overruns on many public sector projects, and far too small a return on many public sector investments. Even though the plans have turned out to be less effective than expected, they help guide investment priorities, policy recommendations and financial mobilization.

6

Extension Administration

Introduction

During the past decade, the Cooperative Extension System, like most public and private organizations and agencies, has faced an era of economic scarcity. In addition, the rapid development of a global economy and increasingly complex and changing social, economic, and environmental conditions at the local, community, and state level have produced several external factors impacting its ability to carry out its mission and purpose. These external factors include:

- Accelerated rate of technological change,
- Changing demographics of the people to be served,
- Increased competition for public funding,
- Shifting sources of support for teaching, research and extension, and
- Accessibility of world's knowledge base to whom ever has the technology to access it.

In addition to the changing concerns and priorities of local communities and states, the rapid expansion and distribution of the world's knowledge base are bringing profound and interconnected changes that are producing internal challenges. These internal challenges include:

- Becoming more customer driven,
- Ensuring cost effective approaches to make the most of limited budgets,
- Becoming fast and flexible to meet changing customer needs, and
- Continuing to improve to satisfy customer expectations.

Because of the speed at which change is occurring, state Cooperative Extension Systems, as well as other organizations, are at various stages of organizational transformation designed to enable them to respond quickly to change as needed.

Organizations that respond to the changing nature of work and authority relationships are learning organizations. The transition to a learning organization, however, is not easy. A major concern is that employees and supervisors often are expected to address problems and issues for which they have limited experience, and they must do so using authority-influence relationships for which they have little or no preparation. For these organizations to excel in the future, they must discover how to tap people's commitment and capacity to learn as well as involve people at all levels in the organization.

A second challenge facing Cooperative Extension is the emergence of the information technology era. This new era has brought radical changes to organizational function and structure. Extension systems that control and channel information solely through hierarchical structures may have great difficulty being competitive in the information-rich global market place. The management principles and leadership styles followed in these institutions/hierarchical structures are often no longer appropriate. New management competencies and leadership styles will be needed.

A third challenge impacting the transition to a learning organization is that few extension administrators are professionally trained in management competencies and styles of leadership appropriate for learning organizations. Rather, they have been promoted to administration because they excelled in their subject-matter discipline, and they learn their new craft by emulating those who proceeded them. While this practice is commonplace throughout the industrialized world, these administrators often lack the necessary managerial and leadership competence necessary to truly transform their organizations to compete in the information technology era.

As a group, Extension's strengths are in the competencies of:

- "Planning and Scheduling Work".
- "Identifying and Solving Problems" .
- "Making Decisions, Weighing Risks".
- "Giving Clear Information" .
- "Training, Coaching and Delegating".

These are important competencies that extension workers must have to design and implement educational programmes that meet customer needs or to assist clients with answers to questions in a timely and efficient manner. These competencies will become even more important as resources and staff become more limited. The use of para-professionals, work teams, and volunteers may help us to deliver more programmes or more effectively use our resources; however, extension staff will need the skills to effectively utilize these human resources.

Several competencies will need strengthening if extension staff are to design and implement customer-driven programmes that are cost effective and satisfy customer expectations. These include:

- "Setting Goals and Standards,".
- "Getting Unbiased Information,".
- "Time Management and Prioritizing,".
- "Appraising People and Performance;" and
- "Disciplining and Counseling."

Federal and state governments as well as clientele groups are requiring increased accountability for the resources we use. Such accountability often takes the form of requiring public agencies to set measurable goals and standards. To meet organizational goals and standards, individual goals and standards must be set. This requires that extension professionals have the ability to manage activities and projects toward measurable goals, manage their own and other's time effectively, and obtain unbiased information about the quality of the programme being delivered and those delivering it.

How to Develop Extension Organization

The long-range objective of Extension Leadership Administration Development, is to prepare existing and potential leaders in Extension, research, and teaching in the rural areas for the transition to the learning organization. To effectively make the transition from a functional hierarchy to a learning organization that utilizes an information technology structure requires a three-pronged approach.

First Step

A systematic training programme designed to develop leadership and managerial capacity, communications proficiency, and team skills should be provided to existing and potential leaders in Extension. Organizations in the information technology era will increasingly rely on self-designed, self-managed teams. Because MAP provides an objective measure of managerial competencies, participants have a better understanding of their individual strengths and weaknesses. As a consequence, participants are able to target areas for improvement.

Follow-up seminars are being provided to participants wanting to improve in one or more of the 12 competencies for which they were tested. Working interactively with video and workbook, participants identify basic skills and techniques. They then apply their new learning in a variety of hands-on exercises: case method, role play, script analysis, games/ simulations, and self-inventories. Participants also develop action plans to guide their managerial development.

Second Step

Extension administrators should continually assess their knowledge of and skills in utilizing leadership and management principles required of a learning organization. While the command and control principles served the system well in the industrial era, the speed and complexity of information transfer requires leadership and management principles and organizational structures that tap people's commitment and capacity to learn at all levels of the learning organization. Executive development programmes should be developed for Extension administrators to help them ensure an organizational structure that is:

1. Customer driven.
2. Cost effective.
3. Fast and flexible.
4. Continually improving.

Third Step

Many individuals have completed professional development programmes on collective leadership and institutional change. This core group could provide opportunities for new connections and greater communications on performance development of the individual and of the learning organization.

Goal of Extension Organisation

Goal 1: Improve Access to High Quality Learner Services

- Extension will provide access to the knowledge resources by being focused and nimble in engaging diverse people and communities in high-quality learner services that help build sustainable community futures.

Goal 2: Invest for Excellence and Impact

- Extension will increase and diversify its funding base and encourage programme excellence through strategic investments within three thematic areas. This will create measurable outcomes and impacts that will be reported widely to stakeholders.

Goal 3: Increase Effectiveness with Appropriate Technology

- Extension will use established and new technologies strategically to increase efficiencies, expand outreach, and enhance and report the outcomes of its educational services.

Goal 4: Refine Leadership for University out Reach

- It provide dynamic leadership. This action will strengthen establishing leadership for the engagement and out reach mission in a manner consistent with leadership for the teaching and research missions.

Concept of Extension Organisation

1. It assembling human being.
2. It helps in organizing resources.
3. It helps in clearly specifying the responsibility.
4. It helps in establishing relationship.
5. It helps in developing policies to guide the use resources.

Thus organization includes assembling of both human and non-human resources.

Principles of Administration

Principles means the particular guidelines as the administrations guide in the performance of their job.

1. ***Principles of Hierarchy.*** Hierarchy also known as "scaler process" where lines of positional authority and responsibility run upward and downward through several levels. In this levels the authority of making *vital* decisions is entrusted with a specialised person located at the help of the organisation.
2. ***Principles of Authority.*** The authority and responsibility should be clearly defined and understood by all persons in the organisation.
3. ***Principles of Responsibility with Mattering Authority.*** Responsibility without authority is just like leaving an individual to fight with a tiger without a gun or weapon. The individual should bot be burdened only with responsibility but also be provided with mattery authority.
4. ***Principle of Span of Control.*** "Span of Control" is such as to permit as much decentralisation of

decision-making as is needed. It helps in attaining quality decisions. Span of control influenced by:

(a) Intensity and frequency of the need.

(b) Magnitude of their problems.

(c) The age of agency.

(d) Professional competence and length of service of the staff.

(e) Size of the agency.

(f) Size of geographic area.

(g) Importance of the decision of supervision.

(h) Degree of control.

(i) Degree of repetitiveness of work.

5. ***Principles of Communication.*** Communication ensures common understanding of organisational values and objectives. It is two way of channel of communication.

6. ***Principles of Organisational Structure.*** The need for long range and short range planning of programmes, personnel and finances require many adjustments in the form of the administrative organisational structure.

Technical Problems in Building of an Organization

A wide range of factors contribute to the unique form which an organizational structure takes in a particular situation. Following six factors appear to be of special attention for building of an extension organization.

1. Increase in the staff.
2. Changes in personnel.

3. Changes in clientele.
4. Changes in the pre-dominant bases of organization.
5. Changes in objectives of the organization.
6. Changes in bases of authority available to members of organization.

Extension Adminstration

Extension administration involve two things: firstly, the knowledge of administration that can be developed by administrators. this knowledge must be reinforced with an understanding of many local, statewide and national factors that affect its application. such knowledge will make the administrator aware of some of the unanticipated consequences of their decisions. Secondly, the skill and the knowledge possessed by the administrator should be used by them in solving the problems of the organization of which they are members. Unless this is brought in practice it will have no utility for the organization.

Meaning

Administration can be defined as the guidance, leadership, and control of the efforts of a group of individuals towards a particular goal. Administration is the ability of the administrator to plan large projects, weld together an organization for its accomplishment, keep the organization functioning smoothly and efficiently and achieve the agreed upon objectives well within the allotment of the personnel, time and resources available, and without doing all the work himself.

Scope

The scope of administration can be expressed in terms of the functional elements indicated by the letters of the word POSDCORB. this word indicate the following:

P—stands for planning.

O—stands for organization.

S—stands for staffing.

D—stands for directing.

CO—stands for coordination.

R—stands for reporting.

B—stand for budgeting.

POSTCORB activities are common to all fields of administration and are applicable to the extension administration.

Efficiency in Administration

Efficiency in administration are very important which depend on the extent of observation of the basic principles of administration. Proper organization of administrative staff, recruitment of personnel of the required intellectual, moral and physical qualities and proper relation with public increase efficiency. Following steps are increases the efficiency of the administration.

1. ***Fixed Hour of Work.*** All work are governed by the time schedule, irregularity and unpunctuality lead to laxity causing inconvenience to the public.

2. ***Red Tapism.*** Much pressure of work load and following the office routine leads to red tape. In it provision for quick vital decision taking.

3. ***Delay.*** It lead to corruption, which occurs due to the indecisiveness of the person handling the issue as the he passes away time on some routine excuses. It must be avoided.

4. ***Formalism.*** In increasing efficiency it may not be insisted. Formal procedure of working are laid down for control and checking the work.

5. ***Obscurities.*** Due to various interpretations it gives rises to disputes and confusion so obscurities should be avoided.

6. ***Abuse of Power.*** The human and non-human resources of the office should be used for the purpose for which they are meant abuse of power should be avoided.

Rural Sociology

Introduction

Sociology is concerned with people and without people or human being their cannot be any sociology. It cannot be in isolation as its main emphasis is on people. these people are not studied as individual but rather in their relationship with other persons. They stay in groups and therefore the sociologists study people organized in families, friendship groups, temples, schools, industrial plant and other organization.

Meaning

Rural sociology is the systematic study of people living in rural areas and who are living by or are immediately dependent on agriculture. Sociology refers to man regardless of whether his residence is urban or rural. However, the majority of the people live in villages and rural areas and follow pattern of occupation and life some what different from those living in urban environment. Sociology is scientific study of people in group relationships. In rural sociology the focus is on people living in rural areas.

Farmers and their families are members of the society in which they live. In any society there are strong pressures on its members to behave in certain ways. For the farmers, some of these pressures will come from within. In all societies there are accepted ways of doing things and these ways are directly related to the culture of the society. Farmers' attitudes and desires are influenced by their society's culture. If it is customary in a certain community for farmers to scatter seed and plough it into the soil, people will grow up to believe that that is the only correct way of planting. Even if the benefits of other methods are explained to them, their strongly held attitudes may make it difficult for to them change.

Yet not all of these pressures will come from the farmers' own attitudes and beliefs; some will come from other people. Any society expects its members to behave in certain ways. No one is seen by others as an isolated individual. Each person is seen as occupying a position in society, and each position carries expectations with it. In some communities, an unmarried man is expected to work on his father's farm; only when he marries will people expect him to start farming his own plot. A successful farmer may be expected to give food, money and shelter to relatives who have not been so successful, or to pay for his relatives' children to go to school. If a person resists these expectations, those around him will show their disapproval. Because most people like to feel acceptance and approval from those around them, they tend to behave in accordance with such expectations.

An extension agent will be more effective if he understands the social and cultural background of the farmers with whom he works. He will then be better able to offer advice that fits in with the culture of the society, and he can use the structure and culture of the society to the benefit of his work. It is useful, therefore, to examine the main features of societies and cultures that are relevant to extension work.

In this final chapter, three special groups will be examined briefly—women, rural youth and the landless. The kinds of problems and issues which may arise with them both in agricultural and non-agricultural extension work will be identified. It should be stressed again that the basic content of the guide is relevant to extension work with all members of the farming community. It is felt, however, that these three groups do present particular problems for extension, which it would be useful to identify.

Rural Institutions

1. ***Extension and Rural Women.*** Agricultural extension services often relate more specifically to farmers (who are usually assumed to be men) and their various problems in the utilization and management of farm resources. Conversely, non-agricultural extension programmes are frequently directed toward women and seek to improve the use of resources within the home and family, or the care of the family's children. This common division, however, is not always appropriate. Many women are farmers in their own right, either because there is no man living with the family throughout the year or because women in some societies have their own land and their own crops for which they are responsible. Even where the head of the household is a man, women may do more than half the farm work.

In addition, therefore, to any agricultural extension programmes designed for rural women, it is important for agricultural extension to work with women, as well as men, to bring them the support, knowledge and skills they need to improve their activities. In fact, over the past decade there has been an increasing concern to examine the role of women in rural development, to understand the particular contribution that women can and do make to this development, and to implement programmes and projects designed to improve women's lives. Until recently rural women have been neglected both in terms of our understanding of the particular kinds of problems that they face and also in extension action directed toward their problems. Most extension agents are men, and they perhaps lack a basic understanding of a woman's position in rural society. This position can be understood better by first considering the three basic roles of rural women.

- Economic, as producers of food and other goods for the family economy, and as a labour force for economic activities.
- Domestic, with responsibilities as wives and housekeepers to care for and manage the household economy.
- Reproductive, as mothers with responsibilities to reproduce family labour, care for children and look after their upbringing.

It is important for an extension agent to be aware of these three main roles which rural women have to assume, since they influence women's ability to participate in extension activities. They also indicate the kinds of extension support which would be of use. In rural areas, women often do a lot of work producing the family's main food crops. They are also responsible for storing and cooking the family's food, managing the domestic economy and supervising other economic activities, such as vegetable gardening or raising chickens, which are designed to increase the family's food resources. Moreover, they bear children and often have almost total responsibility for their care and upbringing. Rural women work very hard for long hours, usually for little reward, and are often neglected by extension services.

It is important for the extension agent to try to understand why there is often so little contact between his service and rural women. He should begin by analyzing the situation and understanding the obstacles which prevent women becoming more involved in extension activities, and should take them into consideration when planning these activities. Recent studies on rural women have suggested a whole range of obstacles which rural women confront and which impede their greater involvement. These obstacles can be summarized as follows:

Cultural. Cultural obstacles are bound up in local customs and religious practice. In some societies, women are prohibited from conversing directly with non-family men. In others, custom forbids them to meet in public places, while in many, women are openly discouraged from participating in non-domestic activities.

Domestic. Domestic burdens are a severe handicap to women getting more involved in extension. Women have a full-time job contributing to the domestic economy and caring for and managing the family household.

Status. Women are generally accorded a lower status than men and are not encouraged or expected to play an active role in extension activities. Poor rural women find it almost impossible to break out from their ascribed status in order to have some voice in development.

The agent faces a difficult task in trying to incorporate women effectively into extension activities. But such is the importance of women's contribution to rural development that an extension service must work with women as much as possible. The agent must never consider rural women as inferior to men. They are not, but they do possess a different range of skills and abilities. Where possible, the agent should try to deal with both women and men at the same time. For example, he should encourage women to attend meetings and demonstrations; but women have different areas of responsibility and the agent should direct his extension activities toward these responsibilities. It is imperative, however, that the agent study and understand the position of women in his extension area, and be sensitive to their particular needs and problems before embarking on any projects.

Although the agent should incorporate women as much as possible in his general extension activities, there will also be a need for projects formulated especially to support women's roles in rural society. Such projects could include:

Organization projects to build up and support local organizations representing women's interests and to encourage their activities, e.g., women's clubs or groups.

Production projects directly designed to assist those agricultural activities which are the responsibility of women, e.g., food crop production.

Health care projects to train the women and provide the facilities required for family health care, e.g., nutrition.

Income projects designed to help women to supplement their income, e.g., vegetable growing or handicrafts.

It is true that to date, men, as heads of families, have received the greater part of extension support, while women have benefited less and have been rarely encouraged to play an equal part in extension activities. But it is widely recognized that women do make a vital contribution to rural development and that extension should support this contribution. The real obstacles that women face must be understood, and extension agents, where possible, should seek out ways of channeling extension resources into activities which directly involve women.

2. ***Extension and Rural Youth.*** A large per centage of the population of many countries is under 18 years of age and the majority of the overall population lives in rural areas. It follows that young people make up a considerable portion of any rural population. These young people represent the farm families of the future, and it is essential that extension do something toward preparing them for that future. The alternative is for large numbers of young people to continue

to drift away from rural areas and into the towns. For these reasons, extension agents should make a special effort to interest young people in their extension work; they should visit schools to talk about extension and should arrange tours of farm projects for young people to see what is going on.

When talking of rural youth, both boys and girls are intended. Although there are no strict definitions, practice has shown that the boys and girls referred to are between 12 and 18 years of age. Many countries now have special extension efforts directed at these young people. Examples include the Village Polytechnics in Kenya, the Jamaican Youth Corps and the Youth Voluntary Service in India. The spirit of these programmes is to "catch them while they are still young", to show concern for the future of young people, and to try to get them started and established in the rural area.

Rural youth presents the extension worker with a number of particular problems. The agent must first try to understand these problems and how they affect young people's chances of self-improvement before embarking upon any youth-oriented extension activities. Extension experience with youth in different parts of the world has revealed the following kinds of common problems:

Motivation. As young people see the neglect and backwardness of the rural areas, they lose inspiration and often see little hope for their own futures.

Training. Many young people will have been formally educated but still lack the skills required to make a living in the rural areas. Often youth is ill-prepared and ill-equipped for the demands of rural development.

Involvement. Often young people feel isolated and unable to get involved in local rural development activities. They have no representation and no means of making their voice heard.

Opportunities. There are too few programmes which attempt to reach young people, or projects which seek to integrate the youth into rural development activities.

Obviously an agent will not be able to solve all these types of problems immediately but he can at least determine to give youth extension activities priority in his extension programme. He should make and maintain contact with the youth in his area, and he should quickly give some thought to developing stimulating extension activities for them. These activities often take the form of a club for young people, with specific projects particularly for their benefit.

Clubs for Rural Youth

Clubs have long been used by extension as a means to involve young people in rural development to propose projects for their benefit. The most widespread are the 4H Clubs (hands, health, head and heart) which began in the United States and which have now spread to many countries. In other countries similar clubs, such as the 4K in Kenya and the 4S in Panama, have been formed with the intention of bringing extension into closer contact with rural youth. These clubs are important as a first step to bring young people together; they give them an outlet to express their views and problems, and form a base from which to build for the future. Through them, young people also become used to working with the extension services, and they establish a relationship which will develop when they form their own farm families and need extension assistance.

When the extension agent considers forming a club for youth in his area, he should give the project a lot of thought and be mindful that these clubs have three main purposes.

Educational. In a variety of ways, both formal and informal, a club can be the means whereby young people can socialize and train for future life. Specific skills, leadership qualities and a general understanding of the problem of rural development can all be useful objectives of the club.

Economic. More particularly, a club can be used to instruct the youth in different aspects of agricultural practice, farm management or home economics. The club can also undertake specific projects designed to provide income for the youth.

Recreational. Not all the activities of the club should be serious. It should also encourage recreational activities and social events, e.g., sports, day-trips and even dances. In this way, the young people will enjoy the club, and will see it as an important part of their leisure time.

The agent should consult people locally before he forms a club, and ensure that it has the support of parents. He should also find a meeting-place and allocate some resources for its functioning. The agent's work with a club is very similar to his work with farmers' groups, and similar issues arise.

Two important aspects are the selection of a club leader and the internal organization of the club. Often the club leader will be a local, progressive farmer or even a teacher. The leader is not a member of the club and his task is to help to guide and support the club's activities. The leader (or leaders) will manage the club, help in the selection of projects and generally work in an advisory role to the club members. As the club develops, young people will need to be involved in its organization. This could be in the form of a committee of members, with a chairman, treasurer and secretary as committee officials. It is important for the agent to encourage the club to adopt an internal organization to provide some structure for discussion and for project work.

Projects with Rural Youth

Project work, either with the clubs or with rural youth in general, is the means by which young people can learn to do something instead of just listening to talks or lectures. The agent should encourage project activities with young people and allocate part of his local budget for such activities. These projects can be on an individual or a club basis, and should not be too ambitious initially. In terms of the approach to project work and to the steps involved in planning and implementation, the agent can consult other sections of this guide.

A useful way of beginning project work is to take young people on a visit to a farmer, or to other agricultural projects, where they can see a particular activity for themselves. Local farmers are often most willing to collaborate with a group of keen club members. In addition, the agent could arrange for talks by other local people, or demonstrations to explain a project to them. It is important for the agent to be enthusiastic about project work and to try to involve youth in discussing and deciding what projects to undertake. Examples of youth projects that have been undertaken successfully in different parts of the world include poultry keeping, rabbit keeping, vegetable growing, handicrafts, fish-pond farming and home improvement.

Essentially, project work should be a learning experience. The projects are not only to provide useful additional income or food supplies, but should also be educational and a way of equipping young people with skills and knowledge useful for the future. It is important that the projects succeed, since failure could easily lead to early disillusionment. The extension agent, therefore, should give as careful attention to youth work as to more general extension work since he is really preparing and building for the future.

Finally, if an extension agent is to work with rural youth, he should have general sympathy with their views and ideals and feel at ease working with them. It might be better, therefore, for the younger agents in an extension service to take on the responsibilities of youth extension work. Young people will need to identify with the agent and be prepared to work with and trust him if extension work is to succeed.

3. ***Extension and the Landless.*** In many areas where extension agents work, there will be farm families who are landless. The term landless includes not only people who have no land at all, but also families whose landholding is insufficient even for subsistence farming. Both these types of family are obliged to sell their family labour in order to make a living. It is not possible in this guide to give facts and figures on landlessness worldwide. The evidence is, however, that landlessness is quite common and increasing in many parts of the world, and it presents extension with a particular set of problems.

So far in this guide when extension and farmers have been discussed, and new technology, ideas and practices referred to, it has usually been assumed that farmers have access to the means (such as land) to take advantage of such innovations. Yet in many parts of the world a lot of farm families do not have direct access to the means of using the agricultural innovations suggested by the extension service. The question "What is extension's responsibility toward these families" must, therefore, be asked. These families present extension agents with an enormous challenge, which they can begin to confront if they try to understand the characteristics of landless families.

- The landless lack an economic base on which to build any kind of future.
- They are dependent upon others for their livelihood, under conditions over which they have little control.
- The landless family's livelihood is precarious.
- They have little contact with extension or other government services.

- They have no influence over the decisions that affect their family's livelihood.
- Few organizations represent their interests.

It is not difficult to see that the above present a formidable challenge to extension agents who find landless families in the areas where they work. The agent will already have to implement policies and programmes; meet targets in order to achieve rural development objectives; give priority to increasing the productivity levels of existing resources; and work with the farmers who have the means to produce more: Nevertheless, where possible, extension services in general (and agents in particular) should give some thought to the plight of the landless. It will be a question of how much time the agent will have to devote, and how many resources he can allocate to efforts to improve the livelihood of the landless.

The agent should at least take time to study the problems of the landless in his area and be continually alert to ways in which he might make an impact on these problems. In several parts of the world—Nepal, Bangladesh and Peru—extension services have tried to tackle the problems of the landless. These efforts have been based on three main activities:

Organization. The extension agent encourages the formation of some kind of organization to represent the interests of the landless, and supports such organizations as he would support a farmers' group. Given the above characteristics of landless families, however, the agent must be prepared to devote a lot of time before any organization takes shape.

Resources. Where possible, the agent should try to make resources available to the landless to improve their small-holding or, if land becomes available, to help them to obtain the use of it. Small stock-raising projects will also provide some income, as will craft production projects with other members of the family.

Motivation. The landless often lack the will or the motivation to try to improve their circumstances. The extension agent can offer his support, show that he wants to give them some help, and generally try to encourage their interest in activities to improve their lives.

It would be wrong to suggest that an extension agent can solve the fundamental problems of the landless. The root causes of the situation of the landless lie in the rural society as a whole, and only when rural changes occur will the livelihood of the landless improve. The extension service and the agent must not turn away from a farm family merely because it does not have the resources to adopt new ideas immediately; extension is for the whole rural population. The agent must come to understand the structural obstacles which prevent the development of the landless, and he must try to tackle these obstacles whenever possible. Most of all, he must recognize the existence of the landless and offer extension's support in securing a more secure livelihood for them.

Development of Rural Sociology

There are many definitions and statements on rural development that attempt to describe succinctly what it is trying to achieve. Perhaps the one used in conjunction with the UN-sponsored Second Development Decade in the 1970s best illustrates the broad nature of rural development:

- The Second Development Decade equates rural development with the far-reaching transformation of the social and economic structures, institutions, relationships and processes in any rural area. It conceives the goals of rural development not simply as agricultural and economic growth in the narrow sense but as balanced social and economic development.

Rural development is a process integrated with economic and social objectives, which must seek to transform rural society and provide a better and more secure livelihood for rural people. Rural development, therefore, is a process of analysis, problem identification and the proposal of relevant solutions. This process is usually encompassed within a programme or a project which seeks to tackle the problem identified.

However, as can be seen from the above statement, the problems that rural development programmes attempt to solve are not only agricultural; such programmes must also tackle the social or institutional problems found in rural areas. Indeed, if the kinds of problems which rural development programmes confront are considered in very broad terms, they may perhaps be divided into two.

Physical. These are problems which relate to the physical environment of a particular rural area, e.g., lack of water, poor infrastructure, lack of health facilities, or soil erosion. Rural development programmes can study the nature and extent of the problem and propose a course of action.

Non-physical. Not all the problems which farmers face are physical in nature. Some problems are more related to the social and political conditions of the region in which the farmers live, e.g., limited access to land, no contact with government services, or dependence upon a bigger farmer. These problems are also very real even though they exist below the surface.

Principles of Rural Development Programmes

Rural development strategies usually take the form of programmes which implement projects in a specific rural area. Such programmes form the basis of most government and non-government efforts to assist rural areas, and they include both agricultural and non-agricultural projects, e.g., maternal and child health programmes. Specialized staff supply the expertise required, and ministerial or other institutional budgets provide the necessary financial resources. External aid is also usually channeled into such programmes in the rural areas.

While this guide does not intend to examine the areas of programme planning or implementation, it does suggest a number of very broad principles which should be followed by rural development programmes. The content of these programmes is a matter for the specialists in the particular field, i.e., agriculture, health or water supply. It is important, however, for all such programmes to establish beforehand a set of principles to guide their activities. The following principles are suggested to implement rural development programmes.

Access. Try to ensure that the programme and its benefits can reach those in need, and beware of the consequences if some farmers have access to the programme while others do not.

Independence. Devise a programme which helps and supports the farmer but which does not make him or his livelihood dependent upon the programme.

Sustainability. Ensure that the programme's plans and solutions are relevant to the local economic, social and administrative situation. Short-term solutions may yield quick results, but long-term programmes that are suitable to the local environment have greater success.

Going forward. Technological aspects of rural development programmes should help the farmer to take the next step in his development and not demand that he take a huge technological leap. It is better to secure a modest advance which can be sustained than to suggest a substantial advance which is beyond the ability of most.

Participation. Always try to consult the local people, seek out their ideas and involve them as much as possible in the programme.

Effectiveness. A programme should be based on the effective use of local resources and not necessarily on their most efficient use. While efficiency is important, its requirements are often unrealistic. For example, the maximum use of fertilizer is beyond the means of most farmers. But an effective use of resources, which is within the capabilities of most farmers, will have a better chance of a wider impact.

Extension Cooperates with Other Rural Development Organizations

Within rural areas, extension services and agents should work closely with the other organizations that provide essential services to farmers and their families. Extension is only one aspect of the many economic, social and political activities that seek to produce change for the better in rural society. Extension, therefore, must be prepared to collaborate with all other such organizations, both government and non-government, and to take them into account when preparing to implement extension policies. The kinds of organizations with which extension services should cooperate include:

Political institutions and local political leaders whose active local support will help the extension agent, who may thereby be brought into closer touch with local farmers.

Support organizations such as those which supply agricultural or other inputs, credit facilities or marketing services. Such inputs must be available in sufficient quantity, in the right place and at the right time if they are to be of any use.

Health services, so that the extension agent is kept aware of local health problems, particularly nutritional levels. Agricultural development and nutrition are closely related and the agent must keep closely in touch with health programmes and projects and adapt his programme to conform to local health requirements.

Local schools, so that the agent can have early access to the farmers of the future, and begin to equip them with the knowledge and skills required for farming.

Community development, whose objectives will be very similar to the educational work of extension. Extension agents often work very closely with community development workers to breakdown local social and cultural barriers to change, and to encourage community action programmes.

Social and Cultural Factors in Extension

Social Structure. The structure of a society is the way it is organized into families, tribes, communities and other groupings or divisions. A person's attitudes, and people's expectations of that person, are influenced by the groups to which he or she belongs; so too is the individual's access to opportunities, jobs and land.

Social Divisions. Divisions within a society can be based on several different factors, including age, sex, religion, residence, kinship and common economic interest.

Age. People of the same age usually have similar interests and attitudes. Young people tend to have different values, attitudes and aims in life from those of older people. In many societies, elderly people are treated with great respect, and their advice is listened to carefully. An extension agent needs to learn the particular aims, expectations and restrictions of different age groups in the society in which he works.

Sex. Traditionally, in rural areas, specific tasks are done either by men or women. Usually women are responsible for household jobs, such as cooking, collecting water and firewood or looking after children. However, in many countries, women also do a lot of farm work. In a number of African countries, over 60 per cent of all agricultural work is usually done by women. Often, women have their own fields in which they grow food crops, while the men are responsible for commercial cash crops such as tobacco or oil-palm.

Elsewhere, men and women work the same fields, but carry out different tasks. In Botswana, for example, ploughing and all work connected with cattle are traditionally a man's job, while weeding, bird-scaring and threshing are done by the women. Agricultural extension often concentrates on men, with male extension agents visiting male farmers. But any change in the way people farm will also affect the women, and thus may well fail unless extension agents involve women in their programmes.

Religion. Members of religious groups have common beliefs and attitudes, and these may influence their willingness to work closely with people of other religions. Religious differences can create tensions in a rural community: the extension agent should be aware of these. Some religions impose patterns of behaviour which may affect extension. Certain times of day, particular days of the week or seasons of the year may be devoted to religious ceremonies, which means that farmers are not available for farm work or for extension activities.

Residence. People who live close to one another usually have some interests in common. Residents of a village will want facilities such as a school, clean water and health services. They will want access to roads and a fair share in government development programmes. These common interests can unite the village, particularly if such interests are threatened. Where possible, extension agents should try to include in their programmes activities which will unite the whole community in a common task. But they should be aware that there may also be divisions within a village. For example, residents of one part of the village may want a new water tap to be put near their homes, while others will argue that it should be near them.

Where there is tension between different parts of a community, extension agents should as far as possible avoid making it worse and, wherever possible, they should seek ways to reduce this tension. If an agent is seen to be working on behalf of one particular group in the village, other groups may make it very difficult for him to be effective.

Kinship. The strongest groupings are often those based on relationships of birth and marriage within and between families. The smallest of these groupings is the family, which consists of a man and woman and children. In some societies, such families are independent and make their own decisions about where to live, where to farm and what crops to grow. These families will, however, usually have certain duties toward close relatives that they will be expected to fulfill, and these could restrict their freedom of action.

In other societies, larger kinship groups may live together, own land in common or even take joint decisions about farming. When this happens the individual farmer may have little freedom of decision. An extension agent would need to find out who are the leaders and decision-makers of such groups, and work closely with them.

Common Economic Interest. Economic differences are an important part of social structure. The type of job people do, the amount of money they earn and the quality of land they own or can rent are factors which can divide society into distinct groupings, each with its own concerns, interests, values and attitudes. In a rural area, there may be cattle owners and crop farmers; subsistence farmers who cannot afford to buy costly inputs; commercial farmers who are interested in learning about the latest farm equipment; and landowners and tenants. Each group will have its own requirements and expectations of the extension agent, and the agent will need to adjust his approach to each group's interests.

The most important economic factors creating divisions within rural societies are the amounts of land and money that each farmer has. This is particularly clear in some Latin

American countries where a small proportion of families own very large estates while most families work as farm labourers or farm their own very small plots on a subsistence basis. Most Asian countries also have large numbers of landless laborers as well as small and large farmers. Each of these categories of farmers has very different needs in terms of extension support.

Economic differences affect the type of advice and support that an extension agent should offer each category of farmer. Such differences determine the standard of living that people can achieve and they also affect a farmer's relative economic and political influence. Large farmers are more likely to be given credit than small farmers, and merchants and traders will give them better terms because they buy and sell in larger quantities. Planners and political leaders often listen to them more readily. Extension agents may also find it more attractive to work with the larger farmers. But if smaller farmers are to be helped, extension agents should be aware of these divisions and look for ways of supporting those farmers who are keen to improve their farms but have not much political or economic influence.

Social Groups

The broad social divisions that affect the attitudes, needs and interests of the members of a society have been discussed. There are also, in all societies, small groups of people who come together for a common purpose or activity. Some of these groups may stay in existence for a long time. A savings club, for instance, may continue to meet week after week for many years. Although the members may change, the club will remain. Other groups may be temporary, such as when several neighbors agree to help with the farm work on each other's land.

These groups can be very useful for extension agents and can often form the basis of extension groups. In the

Republic of Korea, for example, traditional women's savings groups have developed into Mothers' Clubs, which are extremely influential in village development activities. These clubs raise large sums of money for community projects, contribute labour for self help projects, and are a channel for information on farming and popular education for rural women.

People, however, vary in their readiness to join groups. In some communities, for example, kinship groups may own land jointly but leave each small family to farm its own plots. In this situation, any change in farming practice would depend on separate decisions by many individual farmers. Elsewhere, the members of the kinship groups may farm the land together. In that case, an extension agent should work with the group as a whole, probably through its traditional leaders, to improve farming practice.

An extension agent should use such groups whenever possible, and to assist his work he should try to find out (a) what groups there are in the region, (b) what joint activities are undertaken by members of each group, (c) the interests of each group, and (d) whether any of the groups could form the basis of an extension group It is essential that the extension agent in the field know what his colleagues in other services and government departments are doing, and that they understand what he is doing. Close cooperation not only avoids duplication but provides opportunities for integrated farm programmes.

Social Expectations. It was stated earlier that a person's position will determine the way others expect him or her to behave. These expectations are known as norms. It is the norm in some societies, for example, for a married woman to eat her meal only after her husband has finished eating. These norms are deeply ingrained in people's attitudes and beliefs. They not only determine how other people think an individual should behave; they determine what behaviour the individual feels is correct. Extension agents should be sensitive to these expectations and should not underestimate their influence on people's behaviour, however irrational they may seem at first.

Culture

The culture of a society is the accepted way of doing things in that particular society. It is the way in which people live, their customs, traditions, methods of cultivation and so on. The culture of a society is learned by each individual member of that society. Children are not born with this knowledge; they learn by seeing how older children and adults behave. As they grow up, older members of their family or kinship group teach them about the customs and traditions of the group and the society. Later still, they may be initiated more fully into the society at ceremonies where they are taught traditional habits and customs, and their expected role. Experience also gives the individual a better understanding of the behaviour pattern of the community and may teach the individual how to change some of the traditional forms of behaviour for newer, more modern forms.

Culture is not an accidental collection of customs and habits but has been evolved by the people to help them in their conduct of life. Each aspect of the culture of a society has a definite purpose and function and is, therefore, related to all the other aspects of its culture. This is important to remember when planning extension programmes. Changes in one aspect of culture may have an effect on other aspects of that culture. If changes in one aspect of culture are introduced, and these are likely to have an unacceptable effect on other aspects, then a programme may have little chance of success. This is one reason why local leaders and farm people should help in planning an extension programme. They will know whether or not the changes proposed will be acceptable to the society.

The more an extension agent learns about and comes to respect the culture of the people with whom he works, the more he will be accepted by them. He will also be more sensitive to the type of advice and support that will be useful.

There are five particular aspects of local culture that the extension agent should be aware of the farming system, land tenure, inheritance, ceremonies and festivals, and traditional means of communication.

Farming Systems

Before he can offer any advice to farmers, the extension agent must understand their present farming system. What crops are grown and in what sequence or combination? How important is each crop in the local diet? How is land prepared for planting? When are the main farm operations carried out? Why do people farm in the way they do? Farming systems are complex, and change in one aspect may create problems in others. In parts of Nepal, for example, millet is sometimes planted between maize plants. Thus, any change in maize spacing or subsequent weeding practice will affect millet production. Similarly, in regions of Nigeria, up to 12 crops may be grown together on a single plot.

Once he is familiar with local farming systems, the extension agent can explore the possibilities for improvement. New farming practices will be more acceptable to farmers if they can be introduced into existing systems without drastic changes. Perhaps the timing of certain operations can be adjusted, or weeding carried out more regularly. Different seed varieties could be tried, or water use improved to provide more irrigated land. It is important to begin with what is already there and build upon it.

Farming practice is not isolated from the rest of the society's culture and it cannot be treated as a purely technical subject. It influences, and is influenced by, other aspects such as food preferences, land tenure and family relationships. In one African country, for example, extension agents encouraged farmers to plant their crops a few weeks earlier than they usually did. Research findings showed that output would increase and that even if the early sowing failed because of lack of rain, farmers would have the chance of re-planting. However, this advice challenged the authority of traditional leaders. Nobody was supposed to begin ploughing and planting until the village headman had declared that the time was right. The advice also conflicted with the relationship between cattle owners and arable farmers: cattle were allowed to graze freely on the stubble and grass in the fields until the planting season began. This simple recommendation, therefore, had implications for other aspects of culture, which made it difficult for individual farmers to change their farming practice.

Farming Systems

Land Tenure. Land tenure consists of the ways in which people obtain the right to possess and use land. Land—tenure systems vary from one society to another. In some communities land is owned by a tribe or kinship group, and each family has the right to use as much land as it needs to feed itself. It cannot sell or rent that land to anyone else, and there may be restrictions on the uses to which the land can be put. In other societies individuals can buy land and do what they like with it.

The land—tenure system will affect people's ability and incentive to take extension advice. In some countries, for example, land is farmed on a share-cropping basis. The farmer gives a fixed proportion of everything that is produced on the land to the landowner. The farmer will, therefore, be unwilling to adopt new practices if most of the benefits will go to the landowner. Elsewhere, a young farmer may want to plant a tree crop, but is not allowed to do so by the leaders of the kinship group that owns the land. Or perhaps a tenant would like to improve his farm by fencing it or installing an irrigation pump but may decide not to, fearing that his landlord may take back the land without paying him any compensation for the improvements.

Inheritance. The way in which land and other possessions pass from one generation to the next also affects extension work. In some cultures, a man's possessions are inherited not by his children but by his mother's brothers and their children. This may reduce a farmer's incentive to develop the farm. In many areas, it is normal practice for a man to divide his land between his sons and daughters before he dies. Such a farmer will not want to do anything to the land that will make it difficult for each portion to be farmed separately later. In other rural societies, land is not inherited at all. When farmers die, the land they farmed is taken back by their kinship groups for reallocation. Extension agents should understand the local inheritance rules, because they will affect the ability of young farmers to acquire land, and the incentive of farmers to take their advice.

Ceremonies and Festivals. Ceremonies are a central feature of culture. They include religious festivals, celebrations to mark important seasons, such as the start of planting or the end of harvest, and ceremonies for events within the life of a family or community, such as marriage, birth and death. An extension agent needs to know when these take place so that he can plan his activities around them. He should also take care to behave in the appropriate way on such occasions.

Traditional Means of Communication. All societies have ways of spreading information and sharing ideas. Songs, proverbs, drama, dancing, religious gatherings and village meetings are just a few of the traditional means of communication that an extension agent may find in a rural area.

There are two main reasons why these means of communication are important for extension:

- The extension agent can learn from them what people in the community are saying and thinking. An understanding of local proverbs, for example, will give the agent an insight into people's knowledge of their environment and their attitudes toward farming. Songs and dances often express deeply held feelings which an extension agent should be aware of when planning his programmes.
- The extension agent can make use of these traditional means of communication to pass on information and ideas. Many extension services now use drama, puppets and songs to convey new ideas.

Social and Cultural Change

Social structures and cultures are never completely static; they can and do change. The speed at which change takes place depends to a large extent on the contact people have with other cultures and new ideas, and on the ability of individuals within the society to initiate and accept change. Although the extension agent should respect and work through the existing culture and social structure, his task should be to help to speed up cultural change in farming. This may in turn contribute to wider social changes.

As ideas or methods are accepted within a society, they gradually come to be regarded as customary. A hundred and fifty years ago, land preparation in most of what is now Botswana was done with hoes. Farmers saw ploughs being used in what is now South Africa and introduced them to their own farms, with the result that an ox-drawn plough is now regarded as the normal equipment for land preparation and planting. More recently, in parts of Pakistan and Egypt, tractors are becoming part of the culture as they gradually replace draught animals as a source of power in farm operations.

New crops can also be introduced. Cocoa was unknown in Ghana until it was brought from the United States. Ghanaian farmers began to cultivate it in the nineteenth century when traders were keen to export the cocoa beans to Europe. Farmers learned the necessary techniques of raising young trees, fermenting and drying the beans and storage. Land tenure rules changed as families moved to new areas to acquire land from other people on which to start cocoa farms. Cocoa gradually became a central part of Ghana's economy, tradition and culture.

As well as being aware of the social and cultural changes occurring in the area where he is working, the agent should try to understand the factors that can bring about such change.

Factors in Change

Innovators. In every society, there are some individuals who are more ready than others to accept new ways of life. These people have a certain influence, but they can also often cause suspicion and jealousy among those who are less eager to change. However, if the new ways are seen to benefit those who have adopted them, the rest of the community may eventually come to accept them. The innovator may then be regarded without suspicion, and even gain in influence. General attitudes toward cultural change can then shift; new ideas may be welcomed as promising a better life instead of being regarded as a threat to established ways of doing things.

Contact with other Cultures. Contact with other societies is an important force for cultural change. Cassava, for example, was first introduced to the west coast of Africa by Portuguese travellers who brought it from South America. It is now an important element in the diet in West African towns, and its introduction has led to many changes in farming systems. Similarly, maize spread from the United States throughout the world as people took it with them on their travels to other countries.

Extension agents often travel outside their areas in order to study. People who leave their society, to study or work among another society, bring back ideas which may change their way of life and be adopted by other people in their society. New styles of clothing, music, religious beliefs, house designs, political ideas and so on are spread from culture to culture by visitors and returning travellers. The more people are exposed to new ideas, the more likely it is that change may be accepted by the society as a whole.

Communication. Contact between different cultures is far more widespread than it used to be. New methods of communication bring societies throughout the world relatively easily into contact.

On a more local scale, roads and railways have brought many changes to rural society. Travel has been made easier and more people can visit other places and learn different ways of doing things. Traders establish shops and the goods in them may act as incentives for farmers to produce more in order to buy them. Crops can be marketed more easily and farming inputs brought into rural areas more quickly and cheaply.

Air travel has also had important effects. In Papua New Guinea, air services have enabled isolated mountain communities to market vegetables in towns and mining settlements that used to be inaccessible. The aeroplane has also helped to open up previously inaccessible areas of the Peruvian and Bolivian mountain regions. Villagers can now visit other communities and receive visitors from all over the world.

Newspapers, radio and television can also bring rural people in remote areas into contact with the outside world.

People in rural communities who have radio sets or who read newspapers are usually influential and can spread their knowledge or new ideas to their neighbours. Education is another way of introducing people to the ideas, values and way of life of other societies.

Population Growth. There is a close relationship between population size, farming systems and other aspects of culture. Where there are not many people in an area and there is plenty of farming land, farmers may abandon their fields after two or three seasons and move on to fresh, fertile land. The old fields then have a chance to recover during a fallow period. Whole villages may move as new land is cleared and prepared for farming but as population grows, land becomes scarce. New methods of farming have to be developed which allow fields to be cultivated year after year. Villages become permanent settlements. More elaborate houses can then be built because they do not have to be abandoned or moved every few years. As land becomes more and more scarce, individuals or families may move to other areas or to towns to look for work.

Economic Factors. Economic development leads to changes in many aspects of people's lives and culture. The growth of towns and cities and the development of mines and industries have created new kinds of work in new places. People leave their rural homes to find work. In southern Africa, many men go to work in the mines and cities for a year at a time, leaving their wives to look after their farms. Jobs on the farm that were traditionally done by men now have to be done by women.

Elsewhere, on the fringes of the city, farming may become only a part-time occupation. Most families' main income may come from jobs in the city, but they keep their farmland as an insurance against unemployment and as a source of food. The presence of large numbers of part-time farmers will affect extension. Day-time meetings may be poorly attended, and part-time farmers will not necessarily be interested in new farming practices that increase output if it means spending more time working in the fields.

The growth of towns affects other aspects of culture, as well as the pattern of farming. Inheritance and land-tenure rules may change as people no longer have to rely on farmland to make a living. Where a lot of people from a village work in towns, they may be unable to attend traditional rural ceremonies and festivals which may then decline in importance. At the same time, those working in towns bring money and new possessions back to the village. These can improve rural living standards and have an important influence on values at the village level.

Social and Cultural Barriers to Agricultural Change

Although cultures and social structures are always changing, the process is often slow. In the short-term, there will be features of society and culture that may act as barriers to change in agriculture. It is important that the extension agent be aware of the existence of such barriers and to take them into account in his work.

Respect for Tradition. Many rural societies look upon new methods with indifference and sometimes with suspicion. Respect for elders often results in the attitude that the old ways are best. Farmers not only fear the unknown and untried but they also fear criticism for doing something different from other farmers. In such situations, the motives of extension agents and others seeking to promote change can often be misunderstood. Village people may think that the extension agent is introducing changes to benefit himself. Such attitudes explain the behaviour of farmers who seem to agree that a new method is good but are not prepared to put it into practice.

Belief in One's Own Culture. Members of all societies believe that their way of life is best. "These new methods of farming may be all right for some people but they are no good for us." This attitude results in reluctance to try something new. "How can it be better than our way?" and "We know what is best for us" are reactions that extension agents may meet in opposition to suggestions for change.

Pride and Dignity. Farmers may be too proud to practice ways of farming that could result in other farmers looking down on them. For example, they might be too proud to carry cattle manure to the fields. Many young people leaving school look down on farming, even though some successful farmers earn more than most government employees and school teachers.

Relative Values. Extension agents often emphasize the improved yield or cash return that can be gained by adopting new farm practices. However, farmers may value taste, appearance or some other factor more than the level of output. They may also value their leisure time so highly that they are not prepared to work longer hours on their farms. Certain improved varieties of maize have been rejected by small-scale farmers in several countries because of their poor flavour, even though they have shown a much better yield than local maize. Farmers and their families have to eat what they produce as well as sell some of it, so taste and cooking quality are very important.

Responsibilities and Social Obligations. Individuals within a society or a kinship group have responsibilities which they are expected to carry out. People who avoid such responsibilities anger other members of the society. As an individual's income increases, so obligations to society or family increase. The more money a farmer earns, the more help kinsmen will expect. This can be a very serious barrier to change if the individual sees little advantage in improving his or her position because there is not much personal benefit from the improvement. However, this may be overcome by concealing wealth, by distributing cattle among friends, or by burying or banking money so that relatives can be told that no money is available to help them. This may result, for example, in a farmer being reluctant to carry out visible farm improvements such as fencing, buying farm implements and other things which might suggest to kinsmen that the farmer is wealthier than they think.

Traditional Ceremonies. Ceremonies such as weddings, funerals and religious festivals can take up so much time that the farmer may be unable to work to the maximum efficiency. The farmer is, therefore, unlikely to adopt new methods, which, while they might increase income, would mean that more time had to be devoted to working the farm and less to ceremonial and social obligations.

The extension agent needs to understand and to be sensitive to these potential social and cultural barriers to change; however, by carefully selecting what he encourages farmers to do, and how to convey the message, their effect can be reduced. Winning the support of traditional community leaders, for example, may lessen the effects of tradition. Furthermore, by making sure that popular food crops are included in agricultural programmes and that the recommended varieties are acceptable on grounds of taste and cooking quality, the extension agent can increase the likelihood of his advice being accepted. Extension programmes aiming at introducing new methods should take into account the possible effect on the whole society and its culture, and not merely the technical results of the methods recommended.

8

Community Organization

Introduction: Community Organisation is considered as a process involving the total community in identifying and solving the problems.

Community means the people living in a specific geographic area. It includes groups of people, sharing common interest and functions,

Community organisation is a process by which a community identify its need, develop confidence and will to work at them, finds resources to deal with them, and in doing, develop cooperative and collaborative attitude and practices in the community.

The objectives of community organisation is to develop the community in terms of its capacity to function as a unit in respect to its reeds, problems and Common objectives. This process of community Organisation has two aspects:

(a) Planning

(b) Community integration

The whole extension process is dependent upon the extension agent, who is the critical element in all extension activities. If the extension agent is not able to respond to a given situation and function effectively, it does not matter how imaginative the extension approach is or how impressive the supply of inputs and resources for extension work. Indeed, the effectiveness of the extension agent can often determine the success or failure of an extension programme.

The extension agent has to work with people in a variety of different ways. It is often an intimate relationship and one which demands much tact and resourcefulness. The agent inevitably works with people whose circumstances are different from his own. He is an educated, trained professional working with farmers, many of whom have little formal education and lead a way of life which may be quite different from his.

In his extension work, the agent basically intervenes in the life of the farmers in a particular area. The extension agent is a change agent: he intervenes to bring about change in order to help improve the lives of the farmers and their families. This is not an easy task and a series of issues arise in relation to this intervention. The basic role of the agent in bringing change into a rural area and what areas of knowledge and personal skills would be useful in performing.

Principles of Community Organisation

The main stress is given in community organisation is in involving people in formulating and solving the own problems. The principles are below given:

1. ***Start from the Felt Needs of Community.*** The process of CO should start from the felt needs of the community. The community must feel that it should be changed. It is just like the proverb "necessity is the mother of inventions". This situation is similar to one prevalent in psychiatry where pain is considered as a prerequisite to change.

2. ***Discontent Needs to be Focussed.*** The discontent among the community alone will not lead to the organisation of the community. This discontent

needs to focused on something specific. It needs to be channelised into organisation, planning and action in respect to the specific problems.

3. ***Discontent must be Understood by the Community.*** The discontent should not be limited to a smaller group in the community. The feeding of discontent must be recognised and understood by the major parts of the community. It the discontent is limited to a very small groups then it will be a minority movement in which he whole community will not be interested.

4. ***Community Leaders should be Involved.*** It is considered necessary to involve the people of the community in the process of community organisation. This is possible when the leaders of the community are identified, accepted and involved in the organisation. These leaders represent major subgroups in the community and when they are involved in the organization their followers fed that they are being represented through their leaders.

5. ***Clarify Organisational Goals and Working Procedures.*** The organisation will not continue effectively unless it has goal and methods of procedures which are acceptable to a majority of the community. The community has diversified groups with their interest attitudes and behaviour patterns. These diversified groups will together if they find some common goals and methods to achieve these goals in the organisation. Therefore, imperative to evolve certain common purposes for existence of the group.

6. ***Develop Sense of Belonging Among Members.*** The members of the organisations should feel a sense of belonging. For this purpose the programmes of the organisation should include some activities with emotional content. The organisation develops

strength and cohesion through friendship, mutual support, difficult task, gay times, hardship conflict and celebrations. The organisation arranges situations in which the community is brought together. This is mostly done an celebration and festive occasions. These activities provide rich emotional experience and act as a binding mortar of the common sentiments in the community.

7. ***Use Later Goodwill of Members.*** In every community there are good people who are interested in working for the welfare of the community. It should be always considered that all the people are apathetic and indifferent towards the community welfare. This latent good will should be utilised by the organisation for the development of the community.

8. ***Develop Proper Communication Channels.*** Communication has gained a lot of importance. Communication is not only transmitting and receiving messages from sender to receiver but developing areas of common understanding and hired values among the members of the community. Faulty communication leads to misunderstanding. The organisation must develop active and effective lines of communication both within the organisation and between the organisations and the community. The organisation should develop an atmosphere in which the participant should feel free to express themselves.

9. ***Seek Support of Different Groups.*** There will is a number of organisation in the community. These different units will make the community a strong cohesive group. Community life cannot be separated from the life of these different parts. The change agent should seek to support and strengthen the groups which he tries to being together in cooperative work.

10. ***Have Permanence with Flexibility in Decision Making.*** The organisation should be flexible without losing its permanent regular decision making routines. This is not to suggest that the established procedures of work should be often violated. It suggested that depending on the nature of the problem and hand certain changes may be made for the smooth and quick working of the organisation. The organisation should not be a victim of red-tape.

11. ***Adjust Pace of work with Community.*** The capacities of the communities differ in terms of their adjustment with the changing environment. It is therefore necessary to adjust the pace of life which exists in a particular community to keep up the tempo of the community programme. Secondly, the organisation should develop a pace of work by taking into account its resources.

12. ***Develop Effective Leadership.*** In the process of community organisation there is an involvement of the people through their leaders. The organisation should seek to develop effective leadership in the community. These leaders will contribute to the development of morale in the organisation and the community.

13. ***Develop Collaborative and Cooperative Attitudes.*** The process of community organisation is expected to develop a collaborative and cooperative attitudes among the community. While doing this the organisation can become a symbol of loyalty and community cooperation. This will develop strength, stability and prestige in the community. One can have an idea of the community, from the organisations and the way the organisations functions. The organisation must have strength both in terms of its involvement of accepted

group leaders and in terms of its ability to handle difficult community problems.

The Role of the Agent

There are no models of an agent's role which are applicable to all situations. An agent must consider each situation individually and adopt a position or role suitable to that situation.

Indeed, there is a wide variety of views on the extension agent's role in bringing about change among farmers. To illustrate this range of views, a number of different statements on the agent's role, taken from extension practice from different parts of the world, can be examined.

- An extension agent tries to arouse people to recognize and take an interest in their problems, to overcome these problems, to teach them how to do so, to persuade them to act on his teaching, so that they ultimately achieve a sense of satisfaction and pride in their achievements.
- A change agent is a person whose primary role is to achieve a transformation of attitudes, behaviour and social organization.
- Change agents are multi-purpose agents serving as links between government and people.
- A change agent is a person who sets in motion a process of change after realizing that certain changes are necessary for the rural society.
- A change agent is an activist whose main role is to help people form their own organizations in order to be able to tackle their problems.
- A change agent is a professional who influences the innovation/decision-making process in a direction deemed desirable by the change agency.

The above statements capture the flavour of the wide-ranging views that exist on the role of the extension or change agent. It is not suggested that any one statement is more valid or important than the rest. They are merely presented to show the complexities of the agent's role and to stress the need for very careful thought by the agent before embarking upon a process of change.

However, a lot of the ideas about the agent's role can be assembled into two very broad categories. The agent can be seen as having two main, but different, areas of responsibility.

Knowledge ↔ Communication ↔ Innovation

The extension agent is responsible for providing the knowledge and information that will enable a farmer to understand and make a decision about a particular innovation, and then for communicating that knowledge to the farmer. In this role, the agent is seen as a vehicle of knowledge, usually of a technical nature, and as a teacher who instructs farmers in the use of this knowledge. The agent is formally trained for this position and is provided with the technical knowledge and information which he must then communicate to the farmers. In this role, the agent's work is usually highly structured and based on existing government policies and programmes of rural development.

Educator ↔ Facilitator ↔ Catalyst

In the role of educator, facilitator or catalyst, which the agent may need to perform in the course of his duties, the agent is associated less with the knowledge/communication aspect and more with the farmers' personal development. The agent is less concerned with specific programmes or targets and more with helping the farmers to gain confidence, to organize themselves and to begin to get involved in extension activities. The agent's role is essentially to help support and actively encourage farmers to develop their own initiatives and to begin to tackle their own problems.

This discussion can be summarized by listing the wide range of keywords used in extension throughout the world to describe the role of the extension agent. The list is not intended to suggest that the agent must be all of these things. It does, however, underline the agent's importance in extension practice throughout the world, and the many-faceted interpretation of this role:

Teacher	Facilitator	Organizer	Arbitrator
Educator	Broker	Administrator	Advocate
Leader	Consultant	Enabler	Catalyst
Communicator	Intermediary	Activist	Friend
Motivator	Listener	Provider	Stimulator

The above list shows us the diversity of roles an agent can assume, but he must always be aware that the most important thing is to study the situation, analyse the problems and adopt a position which is relevant to solving those particular problems. Thought must be given to this, and an agent must never simply plunge into a situation without thinking carefully how he may best help to change it.

Knowledge and Personal Skills

Two other important issues are the types of knowledge that an agent must have, and the personal skills required of him to do his job effectively. Again, in extension practice throughout the world, there is considerable diversity on these two issues, reflecting the variety of situations in which agents work. How the knowledge and personal skills required by the agent are influenced by the role the agent performs will be considered.

Knowledge

Four main areas of knowledge are important for the extension agent and form the basis of extension training.

Technical. The agent must be adequately trained in the technical aspects of his work and have a good working knowledge of the main elements of the agricultural system in which he is working.

Rural life. This includes anthropological and sociological studies of the rural area where he is working, local traditions, practices, culture and values.

Policy. The agent should be familiar with the main legislation of government or other institutional policies which affect the rural areas, development programmes, credit programmes, and bureaucratic and administrative procedures.

Adult education. Since extension is an educational process, the agent must be familiar with the main approaches to adult education and group dynamics? and with the techniques of developing farmer participation in extension activities.

It should be noted that these four areas of knowledge can be dealt with by a training programme, when the agent can be provided with the detailed information available in the four areas.

Personal Skills

It is more difficult to determine the personal skills required of the agent for extension work, and to train the agent in these skills. The area of personal skills is less easily covered by means of specific knowledge and information and often refers to skills that an agent either has or has not. A vast range of such skills has been suggested; however, these have been grouped together to present a list of the main areas of skills required of an extension agent.

Organization and planning. The extension agent must be able to plan extension work, to organize its implementation and generally to manage and effectively control an extension office and its activities.

Communication. An extension agent must above all be a communicator, both verbally and non-verbally, and this skill is the basis of all extension activity.

Analysis and diagnosis. The extension agent must be able to examine situations which confront him, recognize and understand the problems that exist and propose courses of action.

Leadership. The extension agent should inspire confidence and trust in the farmers he serves, set them an example and take the lead in initiating activities.

Initiative. The extension agent may often have to work in isolation and unsupervised. He must have the initiative and confidence to do so without depending upon guidance and support from his superiors.

Personal Qualities

The personal qualities required by a good extension worker are often discussed. These qualities are more difficult to define but, nevertheless, they are qualities to look for when selecting extension agents. Some of the qualities suggested are personal characteristics, and it is important to assess whether an agent possesses them before appointing him to an extension post. The personal qualities required in an extension agent include:

- Commitment to extension work and to working, at times, in isolated rural areas, with a sense of dedication and determination to get some extension activities under way.
- Reliability, both in terms of carrying out extension work and also in relations with farmers. An extension worker's superior officers must be able to rely on him to carry out his tasks without close supervision, and the local farmers must come to have confidence in his advice and support.

- Humility in his work with the farmers. The agent must be sensitive to the wishes and feelings of the farmers and work with them in a way that respects them as people who have knowledge and ideas to contribute.

- Confidence in his own abilities and determination to achieve something. An extension agent is often left to work in isolation with little supervision and needs self-confidence and courage to do so.

The above areas of knowledge, personal skills and qualities are not exhaustive. They are not presented as a checklist against which to judge the competence of an individual to do extension work, but to show the very demanding nature of the work and to act as a guide when selecting and training extension agents.

Public Speaking

Public speaking is a skill which the agent will be called upon to practice frequently. A principal task of the agent is communication; this inevitably involves public speaking to explain a new idea, conduct a demonstration or generally take part in a community discussion.

Speaking in public is a very useful and effective form of communication, if done competently. A public speech gives the extension agent an opportunity to demonstrate his enthusiasm and technical knowledge. Some people are natural public speakers and easily and competently arrange their material and present it in a way which is both interesting and intelligible to the audience. On the other hand, if an extension agent is poorly prepared to give his speech and delivers it badly in an uncomfortable situation, then his efforts could be counterproductive.

Public speaking represents an important aspect of an extension agent's work and one which he can use to great advantage if he prepares well. Most importantly, a talk must flow well and give the impression of being well-thoughtout. There is nothing mote off-putting for an audience than a speaker who fumbles his notes, forgets basic facts or talks too long. A well-prepared and delivered extension talk can make a considerable impression upon farmers and build up confidence in the extension agent.

While not all agents will have the same natural ability to speak publicly, there is much that an agent can do to improve his performance.

Public Speaking is an Important Part of Extension Work

Most agents will be able to develop a good approach to public speaking with application and practice. The points listed below are a useful guide to public speaking for the extension agent.

Preparation

As with all extension activities, the agent must prepare himself beforehand for a public speaking engagement, no matter how unimportant the event may seem. This preparation includes checking the facts, figures and other information to be included in the presentation, organizing the material in a logical manner and preparing any supporting audiovisual material. It is also useful to check the place where the talk is to be given and to take into consideration the interests, needs and knowledge of the expected audience.

Some agents find it useful to rehearse the talk beforehand, or at least the main points. The agent should not try to memorize the whole talk; instead, he should write the main items in order for reference in large print on paper or on small cards. Another technique is to note the main points on an overhead projector sheet which can be uncovered step by step as the speech progresses. This serves a dual purpose: helping the agent in the presentation and providing a summary of the main topics for the audience.

Content

Great care should be taken with the content of a talk, both in terms of the words and expressions used and also in the logical sequence of what is to be said. The subject of the talk should be introduced and a general outline of the subject given. The main body of the talk should contain the key points that the agent wishes to make. He should not put too much content into a talk; a short, concise and well-thought out talk will have far more effect than a lengthy, rambling presentation.

It is also important to take some care in the use of words and expressions and to adapt these, where possible, to the local context. Similarly, it is important to avoid the use of over-complex technical language or jargon, which might confuse the audience.

Delivery

This is the most critical part of public speaking and demands much care and attention. Confidence is very important in delivery. If an agent knows what he wants to say, prepares himself and says it clearly and effectively, he will probably give a good talk. It is useful to develop a friendly style and to talk to or with an audience, and not at them. Under no circumstances should an agent underestimate the intelligence of farmers and talk down to them.

During a talk, posture and body movement are important. Excessive fidgeting, gesticulating or other theatrical gestures can often distract listeners, although some gestures can be used effectively to emphasize a particular point. The agent should continually observe the faces of his audience and take note of signs of interest, boredom or disapproval. A talk should be a two-way communication process in that the agent should be sensitive to the effect he is producing and be prepared to react positively.

The agent should always ensure that his voice is loud and clear enough for all those present to hear. He should try not to be nervous, and should not apologize in advance for any shortcomings. A positive attitude to the delivery of a talk is very important.

Finally, the talk should be relatively short, about 15-20 minutes. Farmers will probably be unwilling to concentrate for longer than that, so the content should be restricted to the time available.

Questions and Discussion

The audience should be told beforehand about a question and discussion period at the end of the talk, so it has time to prepare itself accordingly. The agent should encourage the educational purpose of the talk. Moreover, the discussion should not drag on for too long, or be dominated by just a few farmers. It is also acceptable for the agent to direct questions to the audience in an effort to stimulate a two-way discussion.

Report Writing

Extension agents are regularly called upon to write reports; indeed, a very common and serious constraint upon an extension agent's work is the frequency and number of reports which he will have to prepare. Invariably, these reports are demanded by an agent's superior and they can often take up a lot of time. Report writing is an important aspect of extension work and should be undertaken responsibly by the agent, but he should do all he can to avoid being overwhelmed by such reports or allowing the demands of report writing to interfere with practical extension work.

Like public speaking, report writing is a skill that the extension agent can develop and put to good use. As a guide to writing a report, the following are a few general hints to bear in mind.

Ensure that all the information and data which will go into the report are available and readily at hand.

Plan the report beforehand and decide upon its general content, format and style of presentation.

Structure the content in a logical order, introducing the purpose of the report, followed by the main substance, and then some concluding remarks.

Keep it brief! At whatever level the agent is operating, a brief, concise and well-structured report is far more useful and effective than a lengthy, rambling one.

Check over the report, once written, and ensure that the final version is clear, neat and easy to read.

An extension agent who can easily and quickly structure his report writing duties will get through them with much less bother than the disorganized agent who prepares and writes his report as he goes along. Report writing can be time-consuming, and the extension agent will want to minimize the time spent on this bureaucratic responsibility.

The Use of Local Leaders

A good extension agent will always try to enlist the support of local farmers in his extension work. In any extension organization, there will be only a small number of trained, professional extension agents within any one region, with responsibility for thousands of farming families. The solution is for extension agents to seek out and enlist the support of local people who have leadership qualities or influence within the area.

Local leaders can be of invaluable assistance to an extension agent in a number of ways. They can assume responsibility for certain activities in the agent's absence; help to organize local extension groups; assist directly in the spread of new ideas and practices by demonstrating them in their fields; and generally serve as a point of contact between the agent and the farmers. By enlisting their help, the extension agent will have a chance to reach far more farmers than he could on his own. Working with local leaders also builds closer ties with local farmers, and encourages farmers' confidence in the extension service and their willingness to participate in extension activities.

Formal and Informal Local Leaders

Extension agents will work locally with both formal and informal leaders. Formal leaders were described as local people who hold some kind of formal position within the bureaucratic and administrative structure. Such leaders can include representatives or agents of government ministries; traditional chiefs or headmen; teachers; religious leaders; political officials; and officials of local institutions, (e.g., cooperatives). The extension agent should try to interest such formal leaders in his activities and discuss appropriate parts of his work with them. If he can enlist their general support for his programme, then his extension activities in the area will have a firm basis. Certainly the extension agent should invite these formal leaders to extension meetings or other public extension activities.

When carrying out his extension programme and activities in the field, the extension agent will work with local informal leaders. Informal leaders are farmers, prominent in their area, who show the qualities and abilities which can be of use to an extension agent. Informal leaders will exist in a rural area, and by careful inquiry and observation, the extension agent should be able to identify them. Often, by talking to other farmers and asking whom they see as the natural leaders in the area, the agent will be able to identify the key farmers whose support will be invaluable in promoting extension activities.

Selection of Local Leaders

Extension experience in different parts of the world has suggested the kinds of qualities and characteristics that the agent should look for in farmers who might be good local leaders. Clearly, an extension agent should not hastily invite a local farmer to become a leader of extension activities. He must give some thought to his choice. The following two lists are examples of the qualities to look for in local leaders.

1. Initiative to take the lead and give confidence to others. Intellect to understand issues and identify problems. Industry and energy, to work unselfishly with other farmers. Influence over others, and the ability to persuade and teach. Integrity and a sense of responsibility.

2. Experience in farming and modern agricultural practices. Educated and literate. Reliable and a regular attender of extension functions. Innovative and willing to try out new ideas. Trusted and liked by his fellow farmers.

The above lists are not meant as checklists but do indicate the importance of selection, and the care that the agent must give to determining the qualities he feels are important. He must then seek out those farmers in his area who match the qualities.

Working with Local Leaders

The extension agent should take great care to develop the qualities mentioned above. His own relationship with local leaders will also be important and he should always try to be available to support and encourage their work. There are four main aspects of working with local leaders which the agent should keep in mind.

Inform. Local leaders of extension activities and proposals for new programmes, and keep them supplied with extension literature.

Visit. Them as often as is necessary enough to ensure that they are not isolated or left on their own. Try to make the visits regular so that the leader can build them into his own work routine.

Train. The local leaders in the aspects of extension activities with which they may be unfamiliar; formal training sessions can be set up at which the leaders will learn about a new practice, how to run a demonstration or how to hold a farmers' meeting.

Encourage. Local leaders to take the initiative and to begin to act with some independence. The more they can become recognized and effective, the better chance the extension agent will have of making an impact in the area.

An extension agent who has the use of the services of a group of good, efficient local leaders has a tremendous additional resource at his disposal and will be in a far better position to get extension work going in that area than if he had to work alone and unsupported.

Problems of Working with Local Leaders

While working with local leaders can be of great benefit to the extension service, there are a number of potential problems the agent should be aware of. The agent should keep a watchful eye both on his own relationship with the local leaders and also on the performance of the leaders at field level. If the leaders are carefully selected and supervised, few difficulties will arise; yet it would be wise for the extension agent to keep a watch out for the following potential problems:

- If the agent spends too much time or concentrates a lot of effort on one or more of the local leaders, then the issue of favouritism may arise.
- The local leaders function as contact farmers who are expected to pass on the knowledge they have received from the agent. This flow of knowledge from the leader to the other farmers does not always work and the agent should pay particular attention to seeing that it does. If the leader is not functioning as a contact farmer, then the agent will need to investigate the reasons why.

- Some local leaders may become overconfident and domineering, and use their favored position with the extension agent for their own individual gain.

- Some local leaders may be less capable than others and may make mistakes and give wrong advice to their fellow farmers. The agent should always ensure that a leader is well prepared before giving him responsibility for extension activities.

The above examples of working with local leaders are included, not to suggest that they will always occur but to remind the extension agent to keep a watchful eye on his use of local leaders and to be ready to respond to such problems if they do arise.

The extension agent is the key element in the whole extension process; without an agent in the field to guide, direct and supervise local extension activities, there would be no extension service available to farmers. The agent's role and relationship with the farmers are the critical aspects of this process and things cannot always be expected to go smoothly.

Extension experience in different parts of the world has stressed the agent's central importance and has highlighted a number of features which distinguish an effective extension agent from a less effective one. An effective agent:

- Spends time in developing the skills and attributes of the farmers themselves, and does not merely concentrate on extension projects;

- Gets out to visit and meet farmers and does not become an office bureaucrat;

- Encourages local initiative and self-reliance and does not adopt a paternalistic attitude toward farmers;

- Plans for the long term development of his area, and does not only seek quick results.

Again, the above are suggested as examples of issues that may arise in any extension area. In practice, most extension agents are committed people, working under difficult conditions, often with little support. The work of an extension agent demands the particular qualities of dedication, humility and hard work, and extension services should ensure that an agent is thoroughly prepared before he begins his extension activities.

Methods of Community Organization

The tree methods play vital role in community organization:

These methods are based on objectives of community development.

1. ***Specific Content Method.*** In this method an individual, an agency, an organization becomes concerned about some needed reform in the community and launches a programme to secure this refer here the efforts are directed at the single goal of securing the reform or objective which the original individual, agency or organization had in mind. The success of this methods tends to be measured in terms of the degree to which the reform, goal or objective is achieved.

2. ***General Content Method.*** In this method the objectives of a group, association, or council is the co-ordination and orderly development of service in a particular area of interest. In this method the effort is made to coordinate the existing service, to extend the present service and to initiate new services to meet the welfare needs of the community. The objectives is not a single reform but a more general objective of effective planning and operation of a special group of services in the community. Mostly the representatives of the different organizations are brought together in the process of decision-making. This involvement of the power figures in the planning process helps in coordinating the activities.

3. ***Process Method.*** In this method the emphasis is not on the content but on the initial and nourishment of a process in which all the people of a community are involved, through their representative, identifying and taking action in respect to their own problems. The idea is to develop a cooperative and collaborative attitude among the various groups in the community. The aim of the method is to develop the capacity of the community in dealing with problems which is on involvement of the major subgroups of the community through their own leaders in identifying their problems and utilizing their energies in solving them. This method is slow but its effect are long lasting as the community learn to solve its problems by utilizing its own resources.

Goal of community development programme:

1. Improve decision-making in local communities.
2. Empower communities to guide their own decision.
3. Improve the social and economic well-being of citizens.

Bibliography

Berlo, D.K. (1960), The process of communication. *An Introduction to Theory and Practice*, Henry Holt and Company, New York.

Busset, G.M (1961), *A Teaching Manual for Educational Psychology*, Osmania University, Hyderabad.

Chauhan, S.S. (1978), *Advanced Educational Psychology*, New Delhi.

Chitambar, J.B. (1973), *Introductory Rural Sociology*, New Delhi.

Dhama, O.P. (1976), *Extension and Rural Welfare*, Agra.

Frando, J.D. (1958), *Extension Education and Community Development*, New York.

Grewal, I.S. (1975), *An Introduction to Extension Education*, Ludhiana.

Kelsey, L.D. (1963), *Cooperative Extension Work*, New York.

Roger, E.M. (1971), *Communication and Innovation*, New York.

Supe, S.V. (1973), *Extension Education*, Nagpur.

Index

A

Abuse of power, 261
Accountable to client, 18
Act of communication, 75
Adaptability, 28
Adoption curve, 87
Adoption process, 89
Adult learning, 65
Agents Relationship, 160
Agents report, 201
Agricultural, 22
Agricultural university, 44
American Council Rural Special Education, 55
Analyzing audience, 140
Analyzing facts, 192
Anchor point, 216
Anti Poverty, 245
Approach, 48
Articles, 237
Aspects of rural life, 23
Attitude, 60
Audience comfort, 223
Audience learning, 234
Audio visual equipment, 214
Audiovisual aids, 81
Authority, 257
Avoid distracting mannerism, 142

B

Barriers to agricultural change, 293
Before after study, 208
Belief in own culture, 294
Block level, 43
Boredom, 66
Brain storming, 118
Buzz group, 111

C

Case study, 121
Catalyst, 304
Category of adopter, 87
Ceremony and festival, 288
Chairperson, 213
Chalk boards, 180
Change activity frequently, 143
Change agent, 204
Changes in rural area, 13
Channel, 76
Characteristics of adopter, 88
Characteristics of innovation, 88
Characteristics of programme planning, 203
Choosing a subject, 229
Class discussion, 120
Clubs, 270
Collaborative attitude, 302
Collecting facts, 191
Common mistakes, 215
Communication channels, 300
Communication of innovation, 73
Communication, 17

Community organization, 297
Community stakeholder, 205
Concept of extension organization, 257
Concept of extension, 12
Conducting meeting, 164
Content, 176
Conviction, 62
Cooperative, 29
Cooperative learning, 124
Coverage, 158
Credibility, 205
Cultural differences, 28

D

Debate, 135
Definition of innovation, 84
Delivering lecture, 141
Delivery of script, 230
Demonstration, 166
Designating roles in group, 131
Developing on extension programme, 195
Development planning, 246
Different target group, 21
Diffusion of innovation, 89
Discontent need, 299
Discussion group, 209
Distracting behaviour, 234
Distribution, 237
Drive, 59

E

Early efforts, 54
Economic difficulties, 247
Economic interest, 282
Education and training, 47
Effective learning, 69
Elements of communication, 75
Etawah pilot, 35
Evaluating extension programme, 198
Evaluation, 29
Excellence and impact, 256
Experimental method, 106
Extension administration, 251
Extension administrator, 255
Extension education system, 48
Extension educational psychology, 59
Extension method, 148
Extension programme planning, 187
Extension programme, 187
Extension research, 19
Extension service in India, 31
Extension teaching method, 99

F

Farm visit, 150
Farmers and grower, 206
Farmers organization, 115
Farming system, 286
Federal and state governments, 254
Felt needs, 298
Field days, 171
Film strips, 184
Finding solutions, 193
Fixed hour, 260
Flannel graphs, 182
Flip charts, 182
Follow up, 171
Form of meeting, 162
Formal education, 24
Formal leaders, 312
Formalism, 261
Format, 133

G

General content method, 317
Generating outline, 140
Geographical region, 238
Goodwill of members, 300
Government involvement, 243
Grassroot principles of organisation, 28
Group facilitation, 218
Group meeting, 161
Group methods, 157
Group structure, 217
Guest speaker, 123

H

Hierarchy, 257
High quality learners service, 256

I

Identifying problems, 192
Implementation, 137
Importance of environment, 241
Importance of extension education, 27
Importance of extension programme, 202
Importance of extension, 16
Index card exercise, 123
India's economy, 250
Individual method, 149
Informal contact, 157
Informal education, 24
Inheritance, 288
Innovation decision process, 93
Innovation, 82
Innovativeness and adopter category, 96
Instructional method, 114
Integrated area, 47
Integrative method, 109
Intelligence, 60
Intensive agricultural development era, 45
Interest and need, 28
Issues in group extension, 159

J

Jargam, 79

K

Kinship, 282
Knowledge and skill, 14

L

Lack of leisure, 65
Lambing, 220
Land tenure, 287
Landless, 273
Layouts, 236
Leadership, 26
Learning activity, 141
Learning environment, 158
Learning experience, 70
Learning principles, 63
Learning situation, 64
Lecture-cum-discussion, 116
Less is more, 236
Letters, 156
Levels of evaluation, 199
Listening, 78

M

Making presentation, 231
Managing case assignment, 133
Marginal farmers, 47
Martadum attempt, 56

Mass media, 79
Membership, 160
Mental peace, 66
Method demonstration, 166
Methods of extension education, 24
Misuse of leisure, 65
Motivation and self confidence, 16
Motive, 60
Multiple cropping, 46

N

National extension service era, 37
National policy, 189
Nature of educational psychology, 67
Need of extension education, 25
Newsletter, 210
Non-agricultural extension, 22
Non-formal education, 24

O

Objective and extension education, 27
Objects, 180
Obscurities, 261
Office calls, 155
Organisational structure, 258
Organization involvement in planning extension programme, 204
Organizational goal, 299
Organizational set up, 41
Organizing group workshop, 225
Origin of innovation, 84
Other methods, 112
Outcomes of project, 207

P

Panchayati Raj system, 39
Panel of experts, 118
Participation, 28
People involvement, 242
Personal quality, 306
Personal skill, 305
Personality, 61
Philosophy of extension education, 30
Pictures and symbols, 79
Planning and scheduling work, 253
Planning Commission, 246
Planning from below, 188
Planning lecture, 139
Planning meeting, 161
Poise in presentation, 233
Population growth, 292
Post independence era, 33
Posters, 181
Practice, 233
Pre independence era, 31
Preferred solution, 196
Preparation, 120
Presentation, 129
Pride and dignity, 294
Principles of administration, 257
Principles of demonstration, 168
Principles of extension, 17
Prober, 138
Process method, 317
Process of programme planning, 190
Programme delivery method, 101
Projected aids, 183
Public speaking, 174
Publication circulation, 238
Publicity, 213

R

Radio talks, 228
Range of audio visual aid, 179
Rate of adoption, 97
Red tapism, 260

Refreshment, 214
Reinforcement delivery method, 104
Relative effectiveness of methods, 185
Relative value, 295
Report back sessions, 122
Report writing, 311
Reporting group result, 132
Researcher's role, 206
Respect for tradition, 294
Result demonstration, 167
Role of agents, 302
Role playing, 121
Rural bulletins, 228
Rural development organisation, 19
Rural institution, 265
Rural sociology, 263
Rural women, 265
Rural youth, 269

S

Satisfaction, 29
Scope of extension education, 26
Seeing is believing, 219
Seek support, 301
Selecting solutions, 194
Selection of group members, 217
Selection of methods, 99
Seminars, 210
Sense of belonging, 300
Service provider, 207
Setting objectives, 193
Sevagram, 54
SFDA, 46
Shared meaning, 78
Shriniketan attempt, 56
Slides, 126
Small group discussion, 116, 120
Social divisions, 280
Social expectations, 284
Social groups, 283
Social obligation, 295
Social structure, 279
Socialization, 61
Sources, 77
Span of control, 257
Specific content method, 317
Stages of adoption, 92
State level, 42
Stepwise, 240
Steps in extension teaching, 61
Strengths, 120
Structure the programme, 226
Supervising demonstration, 170
Support for the programme, 242
Support organization, 20
Symposium, 110
Systematic training programme, 254

T

Teaching outside your field, 148
Teaching, 68
Technical advice, 15
Technical problems in building organization, 258
Technology for teaching, 129
Telephone calls, 157
Tours, 173
Traditional ceremony, 295
Traditional means, 259
Types of extension, 21

U

Understanding extension education, 11

University outreach, 256
Use of local leader, 312
Using the media, 209

V

Value clarification exercise, 124
Venue, 212
Videotapes, 119
Village level, 43
Visual aids, 232

W

Weaknesses, 211
White boards, 227
Whole family, 29
Woolly thinking, 239
Work with people, 17
Worksheet, 123
Workshop, 224
Written programme, 203